Contents

INVEST IN LIVING

GETTING THE BEST FROM MEAT

compiled by

D. SQUIRE & P. McHOY

EP Publishing Limited
1976

Acknowledgements

The publishers are grateful to the following for their assistance with this book:

Valerie Barrett
British Poultry Information Service
Cadbury Typhoo Food Advisory Service
Danish Food Centre
Fred Mallion
Meat and Livestock Commission
David Mellor
Jill McWilliam
National Association of Veal Producers
New Zealand Lamb Information Bureau

The *Invest in Living* Series

Getting the Best from Fish
Home Goat Keeping
Home Honey Production
Home Made Butter, Cheese and Yoghurt
Home Poultry Keeping
Home Rabbit Keeping
Home Vegetable Production
Meat Preserving at Home
Wild Fruits and Nuts

Introduction

Cookery is an art, an expression of one's likes and dislikes—or those of your family. But science and economic expediencies have been intruding on this art ever more strongly in recent years. Deep freezers, supermarkets, bulk buying, freezer centres, refrigerated ships and intensive farming techniques are now part of our life and the art of buying food wisely has become more of a science coupled to a pocket calculator.

It is to help meet today's pressures on the kitchen—the need to choose, buy and cook meat carefully and wisely—that this book has been written. It has been tailored to help combat the financial demands upon your purse by setting before you the pros and cons of buying meat, whether from a local butcher, supermarket, freezer centre or farm shop. It tells how to judge the quality of meat, how much you can expect to get from a carcass, how to store it and the best uses to which the various 'cuts' can be put.

But this isn't just a book on buying meat—for the proof is in the eating. Whether it's beef, pork, lamb, mutton, veal, chicken or rabbit, you will find a range of rewarding recipes that will help you get the best from meat.

Metric Conversions

For ease of use, non-critical quantities given in the recipes included in the individual meat chapters have been rounded wherever possible. Most kitchen scales are marked in both imperial and metric and sets of metric weights are available for balance scales. A set of metric measuring spoons is inexpensive and will be an asset in your kitchen.

Where teaspoons and tablespoons are mentioned in imperial equivalents, *level* spoonfuls are intended.

Shopping for Meat

Shopping is a very personal thing—it calls on both individual preferences and on acquired skills. Even shopping for the much-maligned can of beans demands some judgement, for flavour does vary according to make and, as prices and weights vary, even the value for money aspect isn't always straightforward. But whatever demands are made on shoppers by food in general, meat and fish are the commodities that soon separate the experienced from the novices.

The need for expert guidance is of paramount importance for meat—not only is it an expensive buy, but the product itself is so variable in both condition and flavour that it is not something that should be left to luck.

The advice in this and the following chapters should help you to buy wisely and cook well—and save you money and frustration into the bargain.

Where you buy your meat is a matter of choice and each type of retail outlet has some advantages (if only convenience), but wherever you buy it's worth treating a good butcher like a rich uncle or the bank manager! He can do you a lot of good, so don't be afraid to ask his advice.

How to Judge Condition

The particular points to watch for in each kind of meat are described in the following chapters, but it is as well to understand what affects the condition of meat—what to look for and what to avoid.

Flavour and toughness are not just the product of a good or a bad animal—though the breed and age of the animal are bound to play a part. 'Hanging' helps to mature the meat—which is another way of saying that complicated chemical changes take place within the meat that influence both tenderness and flavour. When an animal is killed to be frozen, it is advisable to allow these changes to take place before freezing.

Meat is an excellent nutritious food, not only for humans but for micro-organisms such as bacteria and moulds, too. On freshly killed meat there will be no visible evidence of these, but if the meat is handled and stored at incorrect temperatures, their presence will soon become noticeable. On fresh meat, given the right conditions, bacteria will develop and produce a discoloured, sticky, slimy film over the surfaces of lean meat and membranes. (As bacteria do not develop so readily on fat surfaces, a well-covered fat carcass will keep longer than a lean one.)

Meat on which there is visible evidence of microbiological spoilage or physical contamination such as dirt and taints (which are easily absorbed by meat) should never be purchased.

The effect of refrigeration is to slow down the rate at which micro-organisms develop. At temperatures below freezing point bacteria do not stand much of a chance—but some moulds will still thrive.

White moulds can be removed fairly easily but black ones once in the freezer can produce unsightly meat that must be trimmed well before use. Even after trimming the meat may still be tainted and have to be discarded. If black mould is ever found in a freezer the cabinet must be thoroughly cleaned and sterilised.

Never buy more meat to eat fresh than you can consume within two or three days—even in a refrigerator it will continue to spoil.

The Implication of Colour

When fresh meat is cut, the surface appears a dull red, but this changes fairly quickly to a bright red as oxygen is absorbed by the meat. This absorption only takes place near the surface so the internal parts remain dull.

When fresh meat is prepacked for display purposes a film is used which allows oxygen in, so the meat has a bright red appearance (this type of film should never be used for freezing meat, as then you will want to keep the air out). This will mean the meat looks darker and less attractive, but the bright red colour returns as soon as the frozen meat thaws and is exposed to air.

Nowadays, it is becoming more popular to prepack unfrozen meat, especially beef, in vacuum packs. This involves putting the meat into tough air-proof bags and drawing them over the meat by vacuum. This produces a dark colour because of the lack of oxygen, but the meat soon returns to its former colour when the pack is opened. The fairly strong pungent smell released when the pack is opened quickly disappears.

The conditioning or maturing of the meat, described previously, continues in the vacuum pack, which has a longer usable life provided it is stored at the same temperature as fresh meat.

Buying in Bulk

Now that more and more people have home freezers, bulk buying of meat has become an important issue. Meat is a major household expenditure (some authorities reckon we spend a third of our household budget on meat!) so if a saving can be made here it must constitute a large percentage saving on the annual food bill.

However, careful shopping, preparation and freezer management are essential if profits are to be made—a mistake can be expensive.

Buying meat in bulk is not as straightforward as it might appear, as many factors have to be taken into account.

Quality. Buy only from a reputable supplier as poor quality meat is never a bargain.

Price. Check what is included in the price per pound—particularly if buying a whole or half carcass. If freezing at home, account must be taken of packaging materials and freezing costs.

Storage Space. A chest freezer will store 20 lb. per cu. ft., an upright only 15 lb. per cu. ft. The yield from a side of beef weighs approximately 200 lb., which would just about fill a 10 cu. ft. chest freezer. So it is important to allocate an amount of space for meat storage and buy accordingly, otherwise there will be no space for other frozen items!

Table 1. Half Pig Carcass

Average weight 50 lb. (23 kg)

Cut	Usage	kg	lb.	%
Loin	Roasting joint on the bone. Often cut into chops for grilling or frying	6½	14	28
Leg	Roasting joint often divided into fillet and knuckle end	6	13	26
Shoulder	Usually divided into blade and spare rib. Blade bone is a tasty roasting joint. Spare rib joint is also a roasting joint, but often divided into chops for braising, frying or grilling	4	9	18
Belly	Economical roasting joint— usually stuffed and rolled. Belly slices for braising, grilling or frying	3	7	14
Hand and spring	The hand is best boned and rolled before roasting. The shank is used for stews and casseroles	2	4	8
Half head	Use for brawn or pâté	1½	3	6

Butchering. This is a professional job and should be treated as such. The amount of wastage incurred by an unskilled hand can substantially reduce the savings.

Selection of Cuts. Only buy meat in quantity if all the cuts are to be of use. If the head, trotters and belly slices would not be required from a pig pack then it is doubtful if the price saving would be significant.

Before purchasing it is wise to be familiar with a carcass breakdown so that pack contents can be checked and prices compared. Tables 1, 2 and 3 will give you an idea of what you could expect from half carcasses. The examples given are merely to give a guide to average pack contents. The weight and cuts will obviously vary depending on the animal and the butcher.

Where to Buy

There are three main purchasing venues and the choice will depend on your requirements.

Farm or Market. The major advantage in buying wholesale is the price— it should be possible to save 10%–20% on High Street prices. However, the disadvantage is the quantity as buying in this way will mean a minimum purchase of a carcass of lamb or pork, weighing an average of 30 lb. and 100 lb. respectively or a side of beef weighing 300 lb. There are wholesalers prepared to sell half carcasses and fore or hindquarters of beef and even if this

Table 2. Half Lamb Carcass
Average weight 14 lb. (6 kg)

Cut	Usage	kg	lb.	%
Leg	Roasting joint often divided into fillet and shank end	2	$4\frac{1}{4}$	28
Shoulder	Roasting joint, either on or off the bone, often divided into smaller cuts. Blade end and knuckle end	$1\frac{1}{2}$	3	23
Loin	Roasting joint but usually cut into loin and chump chops for grilling or frying	1	$2\frac{1}{2}$	18
Scrag and middle neck	Middle neck chops used for stews and casseroles. Scrag for soups and stews	$\frac{1}{2}$	$1\frac{1}{2}$	11
Breast	Economical cut for roasting or braising	$\frac{1}{2}$	$1\frac{1}{2}$	11
Best end neck	Bone-in roast or cut into chops for braising, frying or grilling	$\frac{1}{2}$	$1\frac{1}{4}$	9

means an extra few pence per pound it is probably worthwhile. Otherwise it is quite common for a co-operative of freezer owners to purchase in bulk and divide the carcasses proportionately. Care must be taken when buying in this way to ensure an economical proposition. Price per pound often incurs a lot of wastage—so the following calculation may be helpful:

$$\frac{\text{Original weight}}{\text{Net weight}} \times \text{cost price per lb.}$$

The following is a worked example:

$$\frac{100 \text{ lb. gross carcass weight}}{70 \text{ lb. net carcass weight}} \times \frac{60p}{\text{per lb.}}$$

$$= 85.7p$$

On average, an animal carcass includes 30% wastage. Bones and fat are all very well but hardly worth 60p per pound.

Buying wholesale rarely provides butchering, packaging or freezing facilities—so thought must be given to getting this done. Jointing a carcass is quite a lengthy process and may cost a few pounds for the service. Packaging materials although simple can again cost £2–£3, so it is important to add it into the cost.

Perhaps the main problem is freezing the meat at home. On average a freezer will freeze down 10% of its overall loading capacity in one 24-hour period. For instance, a 10 cu. ft. chest freezer has a loading capacity of 200 lb. assuming it holds 20 lb. per cu. ft. Thus 10% of 200 lb. is 20 lb.

This obviously can be rather limiting when freezing down carcasses of meat, and to overload the freezer with fresh meat would impair the quality of the meat and is certainly not recommended.

Table 3. Side of Beef

Average weight 300 lb. (136 kg)

Cut	Usage	kg	lb.	%
Bones	Soup or stock	29	64	21
Topside, silverside, top rump	Topside is a lean roasting joint. Silverside and top rump are roasting joints, but are also ideal for braising or pot roasting	$21\frac{1}{2}$	48	16
Flank and leg	Both tasty cuts for stewing or pot roasting, but generally trimmed and minced	$19\frac{1}{2}$	43	14
Ribs	Usually boned and rolled joints ideal for pot roasting or slow roasting	$15\frac{1}{2}$	34	12
Fat	Cooking purposes	$14\frac{1}{2}$	32	11
Shin, neck and clod	Stewing meat for stews, soups and casseroles. Makes excellent stock	8	18	6
Sirloin	Can be roasted in one piece or cut into steaks, referred to either as sirloin or porterhouse steaks. The fillet is also on the sirloin bone— this can be either roasted whole or sliced for steaks	$7\frac{1}{2}$	$16\frac{1}{2}$	$5\frac{1}{2}$
Chuck and blade	Braising steak for stews, casseroles, pies and puddings	$7\frac{1}{2}$	16	$5\frac{1}{2}$
Brisket	Economical stew/roasting joint cooked on or off the bone	$5\frac{1}{2}$	$12\frac{1}{2}$	4
Rump	Ideal steak for grilling or frying	$4\frac{1}{2}$	10	3
Skirt	Skirt is taken from the inside of the ribs and the flank. Stewing or frying meat	3	6	2

The ideal solution would be to have it frozen by a butcher—or you can make arrangements to store it while you freeze down small quantities at home.

If the problems of buying in large quantities can be overcome without increasing the price per pound too much, then the saving can be substantial, but a large freezer is essential to gain the maximum benefits.

Butcher. Many High Street butchers are turning their attentions to supplying meat for the freezer and there are bargains to be had if you shop around. The advantages in purchasing from the butcher as opposed to the farmer or market are three-fold. Smaller quantities will be available; the carcass can be cut according to individual requirements; and the packaging and freezing can be included in the price per pound. However, these advantages will inevitably increase the cost.

Always check what the price includes and compare this carefully with other outlets. Check the pack price against buying cuts individually. If the price saving is not significant, it may not be worthwhile taking up valuable freezer space to store it.

A 10 cu. ft. freezer costs about 30p a week to run (1976 prices). If the freezer is half full of beef it is costing 15p per week to store—a thought worth remembering. Choose a reputable butcher as sharp practices can prove to be expensive. Cheap cuts can be substituted for prime cuts—and this could pass unnoticed if the pack contents are not checked.

Freezer Food Centre/Supermarket. Buying from a freezer food centre or supermarket is by far the simplest way of acquiring meat. Both small packs and half carcass packs are usually available to suit all requirements.

Commercially frozen meat has several advantages. The meat will have been blast frozen, a method of fast freezing superior to that achieved in a home freezer, ensuring minimum tissue breakdown. The packaging is generally good, double wrapping being the general rule. Lastly, prices on the whole are competitive, particularly from the larger chain supermarkets whose buying power helps to keep prices down.

Having said all that, it is of paramount importance to choose a reputable supermarket chain—and one that preferably prepares and freezes its own meat rather than buys it in.

Check carefully the storage conditions, stock turnover and packaging. If unsure, make enquiries and buy only when satisfied that all conditions are favourable.

Compare prices before purchase and don't always assume that a bulk pack is cheaper than individual cuts. Buying in smaller units may cost a little more, but it may suit the family requirements better and it gives the opportunity to take advantage of special offers.

How to Keep and Freeze Meat

Having got yourself a good buy, whether fresh or frozen, it makes sense to look after it until you are ready to eat it. More importantly, carelessly stored fresh meat can be a health hazard.

Never buy more fresh meat than you can eat within two to three days, even if you plan to keep it in a refrigerator.

As soon as you get meat home, take it out of its wrapping and cover lightly with foil, or greaseproof paper. Keep it in a cool place. If you are using a refrigerator, the meat may be lightly wrapped in a plastic bag or clingfilm.

Packaging

Poor quality frozen meat is often a result of poor packaging. Meat exposed to the cold temperature becomes dry, sometimes resulting in freezer burn (whitish or amber coloured patches on the surface). Rancidity can develop also, as a result of the fat content becoming oxidised.

Double wrapping is essential for all cuts. The first layer should be of foil or strong film wrapped closely around the meat; the meat should then be wrapped in a heavy duty polythene bag or sheeting. Seal well, excluding all the air, and *label clearly.*

As much of the meat will be used from its frozen state, it must be prepared ready for cooking before freezing and packed in units suitable for family requirements. Here's how some of the principal type of cuts should be treated.

Joints. Trim off excess fat and bone if required. Cover any remaining bones with several layers of foil to prevent damage to packaging during storage. Double wrap in foil and polythene.

Steaks and Chops. Trim as required. To ensure a free-flow pack wrap each steak or chop in foil or film and pack neatly into a polythene bag.

Offal. Treat as steaks and chops.

Cheaper Cuts. Prepare the meat as for cooking; trim and leave whole, or cube, dice or mince. Wrap in family-sized units (perhaps $\frac{1}{2}$ lb. or 1 lb. packs) and place several packs in a polythene bag.

Bacon is perhaps the trickiest meat to freeze—unless done properly it quickly produces a rancid or 'fishy' taste. The most important consideration is packaging—it is air that caused the changes leading to rancidity. It is always best to buy vacuum packed joints of rashers, and then to put the vacuum pack into a polythene bag as extra protection against puncturing.

The other point to bear in mind with bacon is that freezing usually makes it saltier. A 'mild cured' bacon probably gives the best results. If your bacon does turn salty, you can try dipping the frozen rashers in hot water and then drying them on kitchen paper before cooking.

Smoked bacon will keep in fresh flavour longer.

Storage Life

The storage life of meat in the freezer is affected by many things—for instance, the condition of the meat at the time of freezing, the packaging material used, and in the case of minced meat and sausages whether or not seasonings are included.

Temperature is also vital. It is important that storage temperature remains constant at −18°C (0°F), or just below.

Provided conditions have been adequate, you can expect meat to have a storage life within the range indicated in Table 4.

Using Frozen Meat

Many cuts can be used from the frozen state—this is advantageous as it is more convenient and there is less shrinkage. One must bear in mind, however, that the cooking time is *increased considerably.* If thawing is necessary this should always be done in the refrigerator as slow thawing prevents excess drip. Thawing at room temperature must only be done in an emergency.

To thaw a joint of meat you will need to allow about:
Six hours per lb. in a refrigerator.
Three hours per lb. at room temperature.

Table 4.   Freezer Storage Life

	Months
Lamb, Pork, Veal	4–6
Beef	9–12
Minced meat / Sausages } unseasoned	3
Minced meat / Sausages } seasoned	2
Offal	3
	Weeks
Bacon	
smoked joints wrapped in foil and polythene	up to 8
unsmoked joints wrapped in foil and polythene	up to 5
vacuum-packed joints, smoked and unsmoked	up to 20
vacuum-packed rashers or steaks, smoked or unsmoked	up to 20
smoked rashers, chops and gammon steaks wrapped in foil and polythene	up to 8
unsmoked rashers, chops and gammon steaks wrapped in foil and polythene	2–3

Utensils for Meat Cookery

When choosing utensils be practical—it is much better to buy good basic equipment than too many gadgets which may wear out or fail to do their job correctly.

As the best investment in meat cookery is knives and pans, these are dealt with first.

Knives. When buying knives, check that the blade extension or tang extends the full length of the handle and that the handle is held in place by rivets. These knives are tough and should last a lifetime.

Two kinds of steel are used for knife blades, stainless steel and carbon steel. Although stainless steel looks nicer, carbon steel is preferable for meat preparation, as it holds a fine cutting edge longer. Clean carbon steel knives with a nylon scouring pad or a cork dipped in scouring powder. Rinse and dry well.

To store knives you need a knife rack, preferably the magnetic type. This can be fixed to a wall, out of the way of children. If you have to keep knives in a drawer, protect the tips with corks.

Knives should be professionally reground about once a year, but in between times you can keep them sharp with a steel or a carborundum.

To use a steel, hold it horizontally in your left hand at a slight angle away from you. Take the knife in the right hand and place the neck of the knife on the near side of the steel at the tip. Pull the knife down and across the steel to its point. For the other edge of the knife repeat process on outer edge of steel. Do this several times.

To use a flat carborundum place the blade of the knife almost flat upon it. Push the knife over carborundum surface from point to heel. Turn the blade over and draw over surface from heel to point. Repeat several times.

Electric knife sharpeners are efficient but must be used carefully or the knives could be damaged. Use all knife sharpeners lightly and *never* press on the blade. If you sharpen knives regularly, they should become razor-edged in a few strokes—it is a mistake to overdo sharpening at any one time, little and often is a good rule. Don't wash carbon steel knives in a dishwasher. In fact, they should be washed and dried immediately after use. Use knives on a wooden cutting surface only and never use them for cutting string or prising off lids.

To begin with, a well-equipped kitchen should have the following knives:

1 chopping knife—wide, 8 in. blade for cutting and chopping
1 carving knife—9–10 in. for carving
1 cook's knife—6–7 in.
1 boning knife—5 in.
1 vegetable knife—3–4 in.
1 palette knife

1. Vegetable Knife, 4"   2. Kitchen Knife, $4\frac{3}{4}$"   3. Poultry Knife, 4"
4. Boning Knife, 5"   5. Sausage Knife with Prongs, 3"
6. Cook's Knife, $6\frac{1}{4}$"   7. French Cook's Knife $6\frac{1}{4}$"
8. Carver–Filleting Knife, 7" serrated   9. Carver–Filleting Knife, 8"
10. Ham Slicer, 9", rounded end

Later you can add extra knives, such as a ham slicer, steak knife, filleting knife, butcher's knife and so on.

Pans and Casseroles

A lot of care should be taken when buying pans for meat cookery. Don't buy a thin, light pan. These may be good for sauces, but for meat you will need a heavier pan that heats slowly and evenly. On the other hand, beware of very heavy pans, as although they are excellent for long, slow simmering, they can be very tiring to use. For electric and solid fuel cookers, pans should have flat machined bases.

Check the pan in your hand to see that it balances well and is comfortable. Make sure the handle (and lid handle) is heat-resistant and well secured. If the pan can be used in the oven as well as on top of the cooker, all handles should be removable or resistant to oven temperatures. A pan of more than 8 pt. capacity should have two handles. The lid should fit tightly and the pan interior be smooth and slightly rounded.

Pans can be made of various materials, but those best suited to meat cookery are:

Copper very expensive but a good conductor of heat. The copper should be thick and have a tin lining

Aluminium moderately priced, very durable and a good conductor of heat. Choose a medium or heavy gauge pan. It tends to discolour, but this discolouration is harmless and can be removed by boiling water and lemon juice or vinegar in the pan.

Cast Iron heats slowly and evenly and holds heat well, but is heavy to handle. Cast iron usually needs to be seasoned before use. To do this wash the pan thoroughly and then rub with oil and heat slowly in a warm oven for about an hour. To keep the pan seasoned, wash with warm water only, or simply wipe clean. Dry pans thoroughly as they have a tendency to rust. Cast iron pans sometimes have an enamelled lining, which does not need seasoning and is easy to clean. (See enamel.)

Enamel variety of prices. Buy good quality as cheap enamel ware heats unevenly. Generally it is easy to clean, but take care when cleaning and storing, as it can chip and crack. Never use pot scourers or abrasives which will scratch the enamel and cause food to stick. Clean by soaking in a light bleach solution. Rinse thoroughly.

Glass and Pottery best for oven cooking and serving. These pots tend to heat unevenly but do hold the heat for some time. Easy to clean, but should be handled with care to avoid cracking or breaking.

Non-Stick Finishes coatings applied to the surface of a pan which prevent food sticking. This finish does not affect the heat conducting properties of a pan. Do not overheat non-stick pans and always use wooden or heat-proof plastic implements in the pans, to avoid scratching the surface. Never use abrasives when cleaning. To cover most needs you will want:

4 saucepans with lids— 2 pt., 3 pt., 4 pt., 6–8 pt.
1 frying pan—8–10 in.
2 casseroles—1 large, 1 medium
2 shallow oval or round fireproof baking or gratin dishes
Steamer—aluminium with lid and 'stepped' base to fit any saucepan

Chopping Board

This must be wooden and about 16 × 20 in. It must be of a durable hard wood with a thickness of $\frac{3}{4}$–1 in.

Meat Tenderisers

There are several types available. Choose a strong, heavy one. Most meat hammers are wooden, with long handles and a square end with notches. These are useful only for tenderising. If you wish to tenderise *and* flatten the meat, then buy a meat batt or basher. This is a bigger, heavier object with a large flat end and can be wooden or metal.

Skewers

The round, butcher's pattern skewers, are best. Buy a selection of sizes.

Although not essential, the following are also useful for meat cookery:

Kebab skewers—16 in.
Larding needle with ridged clip for securing pieces of fat on to surface of meat.
Trussing needle—for sewing up rolled joints.

Meat Thermometers

These are not really necessary for everyday cooking but are essential for cooking meat from frozen. The thermometer should have a good sharp spike to penetrate the flesh and an easy-to-read dial. Choose one that has meats and their cooking temperatures indicated on the dial. The spike is pushed into the meat until the point is halfway through the thickest part. Keep the spike away from any bone. If you are cooking meat from frozen it is not possible to put the thermometer in straightaway. Seal the meat first at Gas Mark 7 (425°F), then reduce to Gas Mark 4 (350°F). When the meat has thawed enough, insert the thermometer. If you cook meat in foil or roasting bags, push the spike through the covering, but do not use thermometers in covered roasting pans. When the thermometer reaches the required temperature, the meat will be correctly cooked.

Beef	140°F	Rare
	160°F	Medium
	170°F–180°F	Well done
Lamb	180°F	
Veal	180°F	
Pork	190°F	

Mincers

Essential for using up leftovers and preparing your own mince. For pâtés and meat loaves minced pork and liver is necessary and one cannot always ask the butcher to do this.

Choose a mincer with a large feeding hole and different-sized cutters. If you have a suitable work surface the old-fashioned mincers with clamp base are the most stable, but if not, choose a model with wide spaced feet with suction pads.

Roasting Tins

These are often provided with new cookers. They can be metal or non-stick finish. Choose a rigid one that will not buckle and make sure it will fit on to the oven shelf. A roasting rack to go in the pan is good to have for cooking fatty meat such as pork. It is also useful to have a smaller pan for Yorkshire puddings, or even a tray for individual puds.

Other Utensils to Make Life Easier

Scales—buy a known brand, preferably with a large weighing pan
Measuring jug—heat-resistant with clear markings
Measuring spoons—British Standard sizing
Can opener
Meat saw
Meat cleaver
Frozen food knife
Kitchen scissors—stainless steel (those which come apart for cleaning are best)
Garlic press
Tongue or meat press
Basting spoon or bulb baster
Skimmer spoon
Ladle
Draining spoon

Three-prong kitchen fork
Tongs
Wire strainer
Pastry brush—hair bristles and wooden handle
Carving dish—with spikes
Pepper mill
Five-hour timer
Grater—stainless steel, four-sides with different grades of grating edge
Spiral wire whisk
Corkscrew
Vegetable peeler
Pudding basin
Pie dish—glass, metal or pottery
Wooden spoons—the palette or flat-sided type are best. Choose unvarnished, hard smooth wood

Ways of Cooking Meat

How you cook your meat will depend on the recipe you use, but in choosing a recipe it's worth weighing up the pros and cons of the various alternatives open to you. By careful selection of cooking method a poorer cut of meat can be made quite acceptable— so consider the relative merits of your cooking options and select a recipe in the light of that.

Preparation

Wipe the meat with a clean cloth, then trim and remove excess fat or gristle. Tie or skewer into shape if necessary. All offal should be washed and salted meat soaked in cold water to remove the brine.

If meat is to be boned, it's worth asking your butcher to do this for you— though there is nothing to stop you doing it yourself, which may be less wasteful. Don't forget you can use the bones for stock, soup and so on.

Cooking Methods

There are two methods of cooking meat. The first is dry heat cooking such as grilling or baking, where the food is in direct contact with the heat. This is best for good quality, tender cuts of meat that do not need long cooking. The second is moist heat cooking, where the food is cooked in hot liquid, such as braising and stewing and is best for the cheaper, tougher cuts.

Grilling. This is cooking by radiant heat under or over gas, electricity or charcoal. Always pre-heat the grill before placing food under it. As the heat is fierce and dry, the meat must be moistened with fat. Turn meat frequently using tongs to avoid piercing the surface, which would allow the juices to run out.

Suitable meats for grilling are fillet steak, rump steak, lamb chops, pork chops, kidneys, liver, bacon, sausages and gammon steaks.

Frying. Frying is, like grilling, only suitable for small tender cuts of meat. Meat is almost always shallow fried. Use sufficient fat to just cover the bottom of the frying pan, and always add the meat to hot (but not smoking) fat. Turn the food during cooking, again taking care not to puncture the surface. Drain meat on absorbent paper to remove excess grease.

Suitable meats for frying are sausages, steak, chops, liver, bacon and kidneys.

Roasting. Roasting really means cooking on a rotating spit in front of an intense heat. Oven roasting is, in fact, baking. The meat is put into a hot oven and the surface protein coagulates and 'seals' the joint, so preventing the escape of too many juices. When the meat has browned it is best to lower the temperature so the inside will cook without overcooking the outside. When roasting in an open pan there is no need to use any fat; enough will come from the meat. Baste the joint during cooking to give flavour and moistness (but don't baste pork joints if you like crisp crackling).

Basting is not necessary if you cook meat in aluminium foil or roasting bags. When using these follow the manufacturer's instructions. When the meat is cooked, allow it to 'rest' in a warm place for 5–10 minutes for easier carving.

Suitable meats for roasting are: Beef—sirloin, rib, aitchbone, topside; Lamb—leg, shoulder, best end, breast; Pork—leg, loin, spare rib, blade, hand and spring; Veal—fillet, loin, breast.

Pot Roasting. Best for less tender cuts of meat. The meat is browned all over in hot fat in a heavy pan. It is then covered and cooked slowly and gently in the oven or on top of the stove.

Suitable meats for pot roasting are: Topside, brisket of beef, breast of lamb or veal, sheep's heart.

Braising. A method which combines stewing and pot roasting. The meat is browned all over in hot fat and then placed on top of a bed of vegetables. A little stock is added and then the pan tightly covered. Braising may be carried out on top of the stove or in the oven and it gives a good flavour to the meat.

Suitable meats for braising are stewing or braising steak, topside of beef, brisket of beef, lamb or pork chops, liver, breast of lamb or veal.

Stewing or Casseroling. A long, slow moist method of cooking in a covered dish on top of the stove or in the oven. An ideal method for producing an infinite variety of dishes from the cheaper, tougher cuts of meat. Pieces of meat are cooked in liquid with or without vegetables. The cooking must be long and slow, so that the tough connective tissues in the meat can be broken down. Too rapid cooking makes the meat tough and stringy, so remember the adage *a stew boiled is a stew spoiled.*

Suitable meats for stewing or casseroling are: Beef—chuck steak, brisket, shin, flank; Lamb—breast, scrag end, middle neck; Veal—breast, knuckle.

Boiling. A moist method of cooking where the food is totally or almost covered with liquid. Boiling is commonly used to describe simmering. If meats were boiled they would be tough and tasteless. When simmering, the liquid should move very slightly with one or two bubbles rising to the surface. The pan should have a well-fitting lid to reduce evaporation. The meat may be cooked with vegetables and herbs and the stock produced is excellent for sauces, soups and gravies.

Suitable meats for boiling are topside and brisket of beef, salt beef, pork cheek or belly, ham, bacon and tongue.

Pressure Cooking. In pressure cooking the food is cooked in the steam produced from the liquid under high pressure. The higher the pressure, the higher the temperature at which the liquid boils, so the food will cook quicker. The food is cooked in a tightly-lidded pan and the manufacturer's instructions must be followed. Tougher, cheaper cuts of meat normally cooked very slowly are ready in a quarter of the time when cooked in a pressure cooker.

Whatever is suitable for pot roasting, braising, stewing and boiling, is also suitable for pressure cooking.

Rotisserie Cooking. This is the cooking of meat by direct heat. The meat is placed on a revolving spit and cooked over or under gas, electricity or charcoal. Even-sized, good quality meat without bone is best. If the bone is left in, make sure the meat is well secured on the spit to prevent it slipping.

Suitable cuts for rotisserie cooking are boned and rolled rib of beef, rolled sirloin of beef, lean beef or lamb for kebabs.

Salting Meat. Meats suitable for salting are brisket or silverside of beef, belly and leg of pork, ox tongue and pig's head.

There are two ways of salting meat, the wet method and the dry method. In either case, before salting, trim the meat, then wash and rub with salt to remove blood.

Wet Method. Put 4.8 litres (1 gallon) water, 700 g (1½ lb.) bay or common salt, 25 g (1 oz.) saltpetre and 175 g (6 oz.) brown sugar in a large pan. Bring to the boil and boil for 20 minutes, skimming occasionally. Allow to cook, then strain liquid into a large bowl or basin. Add the meat, cover and leave in a cold place for 4–10 days, depending on thickness of meat.

Dry Method. Put 225 g (8 oz.) bay salt, 225 g (8 oz.) common salt, 225 g (8 oz.) brown sugar, 25 g (1 oz.) saltpetre, 12 g (½ oz.) black pepper and 5 ml (1 teaspoon) allspice in a bowl and pound well together. Put meat in a container and rub the mixture into the meat once a day. Do this for 4–8 days.

After salting, remove meat and wash thoroughly in cold water. Soak in cold water for 1–2 hours before cooking. To cook, put in a pan with water, carrots, turnip and onion. Bring to boil and simmer gently. Cook joints up to 3 lb. for 1 hour per lb., joints of 4–6 lb. for 3–5 hours.

Table 5.   Roasting Chart

	Gas Mark 7, 425°F	Gas Mark 4, 350°F
Beef		
On bone	15–20 mins/lb. + 20 mins	25–30 mins/lb. + 25–30 mins
Rolled or stuffed	25 mins/lb. + 25 mins	35 mins/lb. + 35 mins
Lamb		
On bone	20 mins/lb. + 20 mins	30 mins/lb. + 30 mins
Rolled or stuffed	25 mins/lb. + 25 mins	35 mins/lb. + 35 mins
Pork		
On bone	25 mins/lb. + 25 mins	—
Rolled or stuffed	—	35 mins/lb. + 35 mins at Gas Mark 5, 375°F
Veal		
On bone	25 mins/lb. + 25 mins	
Rolled or stuffed	30 mins/lb. + 30 mins	

Cooking times can only be approximate and are intended purely as a guide. Cooking in foil will also affect cooking times, so be guided by the manufacturer's instructions. Ideally use a meat thermometer—it will take a lot of the guesswork out of timing meat.

Veal

Shopping for Veal

Veal is a meat that's perhaps more often eaten out at restaurants than at home. The supply from your local butcher is likely to be much easier than it was a few years ago, but it is still frequently in short supply. Availability depends on the current meat producing situation— when beef and dairy farmers are building up their herds veal is in short supply (therefore the price increases), while at other times the situation is reversed (and the price drops).

In Britain, specially reared milk-fed calves are produced in about four months, but these are very expensive and can be purchased only from specialist butchers; the bulk of this meat goes directly into high-class catering establishments. Small amounts of vacuum-packed veal have become available on the market recently.

Young calves or 'bobby calves' are much less expensive, but because they are not developed apart from the leg, there is little meat on the carcasses.

When selecting veal look for soft, finely grained flesh with a white to pale pink colour. Colour is extremely important as far as veal is concerned, and the palest meat will bring the highest price. Do not select veal that appears wet and flabby, or meat that has become dry and brown. Bluish or mottled flesh is usually a sign of an older animal. On the best milk fed carcasses there will be a very thin layer of creamy-white fat and the bones will be soft with bluish-white cartilage in evidence on the knuckles. The bone content of bobby calves is high and needs to be studied before purchasing as the final yield of meat may prove to be very expensive.

Imported veal from Denmark and Holland is available, and this is generally of good quality and flavour.

On its own, veal tends to be rather bland, and sauces, seasonings and stuffings are used to provide additional flavour for this rather special meat, which is becoming more popular.

Carving Veal

Breast. First separate the rib bones and gristly brisket by passing a sharp knife through the centre of the joint. The rib bones can then be detached and served. Stuffed breast should be cut downwards in thick slices through the joint.

Fillet. Cut medium-thick slices horizontally across the grain and across the whole joint. If cooked on the bone, cut the meat towards the bone from one side then turn over and do the same from the other side.

Knuckle. Carve as leg of lamb.

Loin. Proper jointing makes carving much easier. If you have asked your butcher to do this for you, you will be able to separate each chop together with a piece of kidney.

VEAL

Scrag

For stewing and braising.

Scrag End

Shoulder

Excellent for roasting.

Shoulder

Best End of Neck

A fairly cheap cut representing good value. It can be boned and stuffed or cooked on the bone. Suitable for stewing, roasting and braising.

Best End of Neck

Middle Neck

For stewing and braising.

Middle Neck

Loin

Prime cut for roasting. Can be boned, stuffed and rolled.

Loin

Chump

The chump end of loin is ideal for roasting.

Fillet

A very expensive cut, often sold for roasting. It is usually boned and stuffed before cooking. May also be cut into slices or escallopes.

Fillet

Middle Neck

Best End Neck

Loin

Chump

Scrag

Oyster

Fillet

Knuckle

Breast

Flank

Hock

Knuckle

Breast

Leg

Knuckle

A cheap cut from the foreleg. Good for stewing and boiling. Can also be boned, stuffed and braised.

Breast

Cheap cut, usually boned, stuffed and roasted.

Flank

Good for stewing, braising and boiling.

Leg

A prime cut usually roasted. Often boned and stuffed before cooking.

Cheaper Cuts

Veal Olives—succulent veal fillets with a tasty stuffing

Ways of Serving Veal

Veal Francisca

Serves 4

450 g (1 lb.) veal, boned shoulder, neck, or breast
Salt and pepper
15 g ($\frac{1}{2}$ oz.) butter
15 ml (1 tablespoon) oil
1 garlic clove, crushed
150 ml ($\frac{1}{4}$ pt.) white wine
225 g (8 oz.) tomatoes, skinned, de-seeded and chopped
15 g ($\frac{1}{2}$ oz.) flour
150 ml ($\frac{1}{4}$ pt.) stock
Sprig fresh tarragon
1 small red pepper, de-seeded and sliced thinly
4 black olives, stoned and halved

1. Cut veal into strips or cubes about 2–3 cm (1 in.) and season with salt and pepper.
2. Heat butter and oil in a pan, fry veal quickly for a few minutes, add garlic, wine and tomatoes and boil for 2–3 minutes.
3. Blend flour with stock, stir with veal until thickened, add tarragon and pepper, cover and simmer for about one hour until veal is tender.
4. Add olives and serve with bread cubes fried in butter.
5. Serve creamed potatoes, rice or pasta and a green vegetable.

Veal Olives

Serves 4

75 g (3 oz.) bacon
2 onions
1 lemon
$\frac{1}{2}$ packet parsley and thyme stuffing
4 thin fillet slices of veal
25 g (1 oz.) butter
1 tomato
150 ml ($\frac{1}{4}$ pt.) stock
Salt and pepper

1. Chop bacon, peel and finely chop onions, grate rind of lemon and squeeze juice. Pre-heat oven (Gas Mark 3, 325°F).
2. Mix stuffing with water, add bacon, lemon rind and half the chopped onion. Sprinkle lemon juice over slices of veal and spread with stuffing. Roll meat and tie securely with string.
3. Heat butter and fry remaining onion until transparent. Add veal and brown on all sides. Pour off excess fat.
4. Peel and chop tomato. Place veal mixture, tomato and stock in a casserole. Season. Cover and cook in oven for 50 minutes.

Fillets of Veal

Serves 6

500 g (1¼ lb.) fillet of veal
1 egg
2 pinches parsley, finely chopped
1 pinch thyme
10 ml (2 teaspoons) grated lemon
   rind
5 ml (1 teaspoon) lemon juice
Breadcrumbs
50 g (2 oz.) butter
Bacon rolls
Mashed potatoes

Sauce

12 g (½ oz.) flour
300 ml (½ pt.) white stock
2½ ml (½ teaspoon) lemon juice
1 beef stock cube
Salt and pepper
15–30 ml (1–2 tablespoons) cream

1. Cut the veal into slices 1 cm (½ in.)
   thick. Cut each slice into 'rounds'
   5 cm (2 in.) in diameter, and beat
   them with a wooden spoon.
2. Beat the egg and add the parsley,
   thyme, lemon rinds and lemon juice.
   Soak the fillets in the mixture for
   30 minutes, then sprinkle with breadcrumbs.
3. Fry in hot fat until golden brown on
   both sides. Reduce temperature and
   cook for about a further five to six
   minutes.
4. Place on a serving dish to keep hot
   together with the fried bacon rolls.
5. For the sauce, add the flour to the
   fat remaining in the pan and fry
   lightly. Add the stock, stirring, then
   the lemon juice, beef cube dissolved

in water, seasoning and simmer for
five minutes. Add the cream.
6. Pour the sauce over the fillets of veal
   and bacon rolls, encircling them
   with mashed potatoes.

Devilled Veal Ribs

Serves 4

¾–1 kg (1½–2 lb.) veal breast, boned
Salt and pepper
1 small onion
30 ml (2 tablespoons) oil
30 ml (2 tablespoons) tomato ketchup
15 ml (1 tablespoon) vinegar
5 ml (1 teaspoon) made mustard
10 ml (2 teaspoons) Worcester sauce
10 ml (2 teaspoons) brown sugar
2 pinches ground ginger
150 ml (¼ pt.) stock

1. Cut veal into 1 cm (½ in.) thick slices.
   Season well with salt and pepper
   and lay flat in a shallow dish.
2. Peel and finely chop onion. Heat oil
   in a saucepan, fry onion quickly in it
   without browning. Stir in all the
   other ingredients and pour over veal.
3. Prepare oven (Gas Mark 7, 425°F).
   Cover the veal, and marinade for
   about two hours, turning the veal
   from time to time. Lift veal out of
   marinade, put it into a roasting tin
   and cook for 20 minutes.
4. Reduce oven heat (Gas Mark 5,
   375°F), and continue cooking for
   50 minutes to one hour.
5. Boil remaining marinade juices with
   liquid in the roasting tin and serve
   poured over the veal ribs.
6. Serve with jacket baked potatoes,
   rice, pasta or chunky bread and
   salad.

BEEF

Ribs

Usually boned and rolled joints, ideal for pot roasting or slow roasting.

Skirt

Skirt is taken from the inside of the ribs and the flank. Stewing or frying meat.

Rump

Ideal steak for grilling or frying meat.

Sirloin

Can be roasted in one piece or cut into steaks, referred to either as sirloin or porterhouse steaks. The fillet is also on the sirloin bone, and this can either be roasted whole or sliced for steaks.

Chuck and Blade

Braising steak for stews, casseroles, pies and puddings.

Topside and Silverside

Topside is a lean roasting joint. Silverside will also roast, but is ideal for braising or pot roasting.

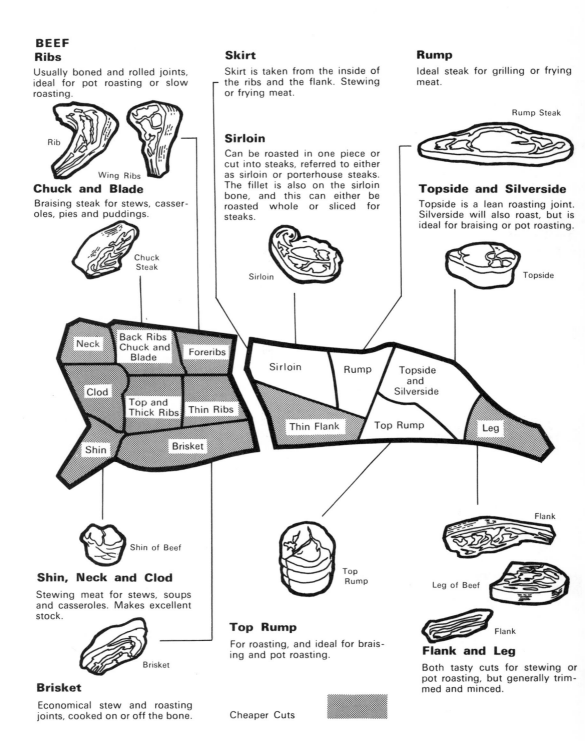

Shin, Neck and Clod

Stewing meat for stews, soups and casseroles. Makes excellent stock.

Top Rump

For roasting, and ideal for braising and pot roasting.

Flank and Leg

Both tasty cuts for stewing or pot roasting, but generally trimmed and minced.

Brisket

Economical stew and roasting joints, cooked on or off the bone.

Cheaper Cuts

Beef

Shopping for Beef

Beef, a very 'British' meat, traditionally comes from young steers (castrates) and heifers, although young bulls which grow faster than steers or heifers also produce excellent beef if properly fed and managed.

The average beef animal is produced within 15–30 months, depending on the system of production used. In the past when older animals were slaughtered, fairly long periods of hanging and maturing were considered essential, but as younger animals are now being used this time can be greatly reduced.

Quality in the beef carcass can be identified by good muscular development throughout—particularly in the buttocks, rump and loin. These are the expensive parts of the carcass and produce the steaks and roasts.

The colour of lean meat should be cherry red and may have an interlacing of intramuscular fat called 'marbling' (small flecks of fat through the lean). This is present in the traditional early maturing quality animals such as the Aberdeen Angus, but is not so obvious in many of the later maturing breeds which produce excellent beef even though the lean meat may be somewhat coarse in texture.

The lean meat should be covered with a light layer of creamy white to pale yellow fat. The bones of the young carcass will be pinkish with a blue tinge, but as the animal ages they will become harder and appear whiter. Dark red sinewy meat with a thick gristle between lean meat and fat layer indicates carcass that is not of the best quality and will probably be tough.

The carcass is divided into cuts or joints which will need different methods of cooking. During life the animal uses some muscles more than others and these contain more gristle so will require more cooking.

The toughest joints will require cooking by wet heat for long periods (stewing and casseroling), the intermediate by braising and the tenderest by dry heat for comparatively short periods (roasting and grilling). Good beef is always available but prices generally are lower in the autumn when many farmers reduce their stock. The prices then rise throughout the winter, reaching peaks in the spring and early summer.

Carving Beef

Boneless joints of meat should be carved across the grain—which usually means horizontally. A long piece of roasted fillet, however, is best carved downwards. Leave the string or skewers on rolled joints until you have carved down to them—and even then only remove enough to allow further carving to the next string or skewer.

Brisket with Onions—a dish with real 'man' appeal

Joints on the bone need to be carved from the outside towards the bone, giving a gentle upturn to the knife when the bone is reached.

Sirloin should be placed with the fillet uppermost. After removing the strings, carve towards the bone and loosen from the bone with the tip of knife.

Rib needs to be placed on the edge of the bone and sliced downwards along the length of the joint, using a fork to steady the slices. It is a good idea to cut between the meat and the bone first if this is possible.

Brisket is simply cut evenly across the bone along its length, slicing the whole width of the joint.

Round of beef needs a sharp thin-bladed knife for successful carving. Start by cutting off a thick round, then carve to required thickness.

Aitchbone should be set on its wide, flat base. Make small slices towards the bone until a thick slice is being cut across the whole joint.

Ways of Serving Beef

Chilli Con Carne

Serves 4–5

100 g (4 oz.) red kidney beans
2 onions
45 ml (3 tablespoons) olive oil
700 g (1½ lb.) minced beef
15 ml (1 tablespoon) tomato purée
150 ml (¼ pt.) stock
2½ ml (½ level teaspoon) chilli powder
Large pinch salt

1. Soak beans overnight in cold water with a pinch of bicarbonate of soda.
2. Peel and chop onions. Fry in olive oil until soft. Add beef and fry for five minutes. Add tomato purée, beans, stock, chilli powder and salt. Stir well.
3. Bring to boil, cover, reduce heat and simmer for 2–2½ hours, or until tender.

Steak and Onion Pie

Serves 4–6

700 g (1½ lb.) chuck steak or skirt
15 ml (1 tablespoon) seasoned flour
50 g (2 oz.) dripping
2 onions
100 g (4 oz.) mushrooms
300 ml (½ pt.) stock
225 g (½ lb.) puff pastry
1 egg

1. Cut meat into 25 mm (1 in.) cubes. Coat in seasoned flour and fry in hot dripping until brown. Remove from frying pan and put into saucepan.
2. Peel and slice onions and mushrooms. Fry onion until soft, add mushrooms and fry for further 2–3 minutes. Add to meat.
3. Pour in stock, cover and simmer for 1½ hours, or until the meat is tender.
4. Prepare oven (Gas Mark 7, 425°F).
5. Transfer the meat mixture to a two-pint pie dish, cover with pastry, seal the edges, then glaze with beaten egg. Bake near top of oven for 20 minutes. Reduce heat to Gas Mark 4 (350°F) and cook for a further 20 minutes.

Brisket with Onions

Serves 6–8

6–8 onions
25 g (1 oz.) dripping
1½ kg (3 lb.) rolled brisket

Stuffing

3 rashers streaky bacon
Onion cores
15 ml (1 tablespoon) breadcrumbs
Salt and pepper
25 g (1 oz.) melted butter

1. Remove 'cores' from the onions, reserving these for the stuffing mixture.
2. Mix stuffing ingredients together, chopping bacon and onion 'cores'.
3. Prepare oven (Gas Mark 8, 450°F).
4. Heat dripping in frying pan and brown meat on all sides. Wrap loosely in two layers of foil, sealing edges firmly. Place in dry meat tin and cook for two hours. Bake onions for final 40 minutes on lower shelf.
5. Serve brisket with onions and juices from foil.

Cornflake Mince

Serves 4

1 large onion
45 ml (3 tablespoons) oil
450 g (1 lb.) minced beef
30 ml (2 tablespoons) tomato ketchup
50 g (2 oz.) sultanas
Salt and pepper
425 (15 oz.) can baked beans
50 g (2 oz.) cornflakes
50 g (2 oz. butter

1. Prepare oven (Gas Mark 5, 375°F). Peel and chop onion and fry in oil until soft.
2. Add mince and fry for five minutes, then stir in ketchup, sultanas and seasoning.
3. Empty baked beans into a casserole and add mince mixture.
4. Toss cornflakes in melted butter and put on top of mince.
5. Bake in oven for 30 minutes.

Oriental Beef

Serves 4

1 green pepper
1 onion
450 g (1 lb.) top rump or thick flank beef
50 g (2 oz.) butter
100 g (4 oz.) mushrooms
1 clove garlic

Sauce

50 g (2 oz.) sugar
300 ml (½ pt.) stock
45 ml (3 tablespoons) vinegar
30 ml (2 tablespoons) sherry
2½ ml (½ teaspoon) soy sauce
15 ml (1 tablespoon) cornflour
30 ml (2 tablespoons) water

1. De-seed green pepper and cut into 1 cm (½ in.) squares then boil pieces for 10 minutes. Peel and chop onion and cut beef into thin strips. Fry in butter for five minutes, turning frequently.
2. Add mushrooms and crushed garlic and fry for a further five minutes. Keep warm.
3. Make sauce: dissolve sugar in stock, then add all ingredients except corn-

flour and water. Blend cornflour to a smooth cream and add to main liquid. Boil gently for two to three minutes, stirring continuously.
4. Add drained pepper and sauce to fying pan and mix thoroughly.
5. Serve with boiled or fried rice.

Beef Pot-Roast

Serves 4–6

25 g (1 oz.) dripping
1 kg (2 lb.) rolled back-ribs or shoulder of beef
1 small onion
6 rashers of streaky bacon
150 ml ($\frac{1}{4}$ pt.) brown ale
Salt and pepper
150 ml (1 tablespoon) cornflour
30 ml (2 tablespoons) cold water

1. Heat dripping in frying pan and brown meat on all sides.
2. Peel and chop onion and arrange in bottom of a deep pan, together with rashers of bacon. Add beef, ale and seasoning.
3. Cover pan and simmer until meat is tender, then remove meat and slice.
4. Blend cornflour with water and add to cooking liquid, simmer, strain and pour over the meat.

Crunchy Meat Loaf

Serves 4–6

225 g (8 oz.) streaky bacon
1 large onion
1 clove of garlic
450 g (1 lb.) minced beef
225 g (8 oz.) lambs' liver
15 ml (1 tablespoon) Worcester sauce
5 ml (1 teaspoon) made mustard
Salt and pepper

Pinch of mixed dried herbs
30 ml (2 tablespoons) instant milk powder
1 large packet instant mashed potato pieces
50 g (2 oz.) crushed cornflakes

1. Prepare oven (Gas Mark 4, 350°F). Remove bacon rind, skin and chop onion, crush garlic then mince these ingredients with the minced beef and liver to give a finer texture. Add all the seasonings and the milk powder.
2. Make up instant potato as directed on the packet, add one-third to the meat, mix well then press into a 2 lb. loaf tin. Cover with foil and stand in a small roasting tin, half filled with water.
3. Cook in oven for about two hours. Take out from oven, cool and refrigerate.
4. Turn meat loaf out of the tin, spread with remaining potato and cover with crushed cornflakes. Serve with a selection of vegetables or salad.

Farmhouse Pie

Serves 5–6

1 small onion
350 g ($\frac{3}{4}$ lb.) minced beef
50 g (2 oz.) mushrooms
30 ml (2 tablespoons) cooking oil
Salt and pepper
Large packet of instant mashed potato
Melted butter
50 g (2 oz.) grated cheese

1. Prepare oven (Gas Mark 7, 425°F). Chop and lightly fry the onion, together with minced beef and mushrooms in the oil for about 15 minutes

until lightly browned. Stir in the seasoning.

2. Make up instant mashed potato as directed on the packet and divide in half. Grease an 8 in. ove proof plate and press on half of the potato, which should line the plate rather like pastry. Pile mince in the middle. Place the remaining potato over the top and press flat. Brush with melted butter and sprinkle on the grated cheese.

3. Bake in oven for about 30 minutes. If the mince and potato are both hot, for speed the pie can be browned under a grill and then served immediately.

Hungarian Goulash

Serves 5–6

50–75 g (2–3 oz.) butter
700 g (1½ lb.) beef
225 g (8 oz.) veal
450 g (1 lb.) onions
5 ml (1 teaspoon) salt
10 ml (2 teaspoons) paprika pepper
142 g (5 oz.) tin of tomatoes
450 g (1 lb.) potatoes
Parsley

1. Heat butter in pan, cut meat into small pieces, peel and slice onions finely.

2. Fry meat and onions until golden brown, add seasonings and tomatoes and simmer gently for about 30 minutes.

3. Add sliced potatoes, then continue cooking for another 1–1½ hours, until meat and potatoes are tender.

4. Garnish with chopped parsley.

Hamburger Rolls

Makes 4 rolls

1 large onion
25 g (1 oz.) lard
225 g (8 oz.) minced beef
2½ ml (½ teaspoon) curry powder
15 ml (1 tablespoon) flour
156 g (5½ oz.) tin condensed
   vegetable soup
Salt and pepper
4 soft rolls

1. Peel and chop onion into very fine pieces.

2. Melt the lard in a saucepan, gently cooking the onion until tender. Stir in the minced beef and curry powder. Mix well and cook until brown.

3. Sprinkle the flour over the meat, stirring, and cook until flour is brown.

4. Add the soup and seasoning, stir and cover.

5. Simmer gently until meat is tender, usually 25–35 minutes and the mixture thickens.

6. Cut the soft rolls in half and fill with the hamburger mixture.

Shepherd's Pie

Serves 3–4

450 g (1 lb.) potatoes
30 ml (2 tablespoons) milk
12 g (½ oz.) butter
Salt and pepper
1 onion
Cooking fat
225 g (8 oz.) minced beef
Stock
15 ml (1 tablespoon) parsley

1. Prepare oven (Gas Mark 5, 375°F).
2. Boil potatoes, drain and mash with milk, butter and seasoning.
3. Peel, slice and fry the onion in cooking fat for five minutes and then mix in minced beef, with a little stock, seasoning and parsley.
4. Put the meat mixture into an oven-proof dish and cover the top with mashed potato.
5. Mark the potato with a fork and bake for 25–35 minutes on the top shelf of the oven, until surface is crisp and brown.

Beef Moussaka

Serves 4–5

225 g (8 oz.) onions
450 g (1 lb.) minced beef
1 beef stock cube
5 ml (1 teaspoon) cinnamon
15 ml (1 tablespoon) parsley
Salt and pepper
439 g ($15\frac{1}{2}$ oz.) can tomatoes
1 kg (2 lb.) potatoes
25 g (1 oz.) margarine
25 g (1 oz.) plain flour
300 ml ($\frac{1}{2}$ pt.) milk
40 g ($1\frac{1}{2}$ oz.) cheese, grated
1 egg

1. Prepare oven (Gas Mark 5, 375°F).
2. Grease a four pint casserole dish.
3. Peel and slice onions and fry minced beef until fat is released Stir occasionally. Add onions and fry for a further three minutes.
4. Crumble and mix in beef cube and add cinnamon, chopped parsley, and seasoning. Remove from heat.
5. Strain and slice tomatoes. Preserve the liquid. Wash, peel and thinly slice the potatoes. Place potatoes and meat mixture in layers in the casserole, starting and finishing with the potatoes. Pour the tomato liquid over the top.
6. Melt margarine in a saucepan, add flour and cook very gently for three minutes. Stir in milk and bring to the boil, stirring, for three minutes. Remove from heat.
7. Beat into this mixture the grated cheese, egg, salt and pepper.
8. Pour this mixture over the potato in the casserole dish and cover with a lid. Place the casserole in the centre of the oven for about one hour, then remove lid and cook, uncovered, for a further 30 minutes.

Steak and Kidney Pudding

Serves 4

450 g (1 lb.) stewing steak
100 g (4 oz.) ox kidney
30 ml (2 tablespoons) plain flour
Salt and pepper

Suet Pastry

225 g (8 oz.) self-raising flour
5 ml (1 teaspoon) salt
100 g (4 oz.) shredded suet
150 ml ($\frac{1}{4}$ pt.) cold water

1. Prepare a steamer. Grease a $1\frac{1}{2}$ pint basin and a double thickness of grease-proof paper to cover.
2. Cut steak and kidney into pieces. Mix plain flour, salt and pepper and coat meat.
3. Place self-raising flour and salt in a bowl. Stir in suet and mix with water to make a soft dough. It should not be sticky.

4. Cut off one-third of pastry and roll out to size of top of the basin, to form the lid. Roll out remainder and line basin.
5. Fill lined basin with meat to come halfway up. Place on lid and seal edges.
6. Cover the pudding and tie it down securely with string.
7. Cook for 3–3½ hours, then remove cover and turn out pudding on to a warmed serving dish.

Beef and Tomato Stew

(in a pressure cooker)

Serves 4

700 g (1½ lb.) stewing steak
25 g (1 oz.) plain flour
5 ml (1 teaspoon) salt
2½ ml (½ teaspoon) pepper
5 ml (1 teaspoon) paprika
1 onion
3 sticks of celery
700 g (1½ lb.) potatoes
25 g (1 oz.) lard
396 g (14 oz.) can peeled tomatoes
5 ml (1 teaspoon) granulated sugar
1 bay leaf

1. Cut meat into two to three cm (1 in.) cubes, discarding fat and gristle. Mix flour, salt, pepper and paprika and coat meat.
2. Peel and slice onion. Wash, trim and slice celery. Wash and peel potatoes and cut up, placing in a bowl of cold water.
3. Remove the trivet from the pressure cooker. Melt lard in the cooker, add meat, onion and celery and fry for four to five minutes. Stir in remaining flour, tomatoes, sugar, bay leaf and 150 ml (¼ pt.) water.

4. Cover cooker and bring up to 15 lb. pressure and cook for 30 minutes. Reduce pressure by placing cooker in a bowl of cold water. Drain potatoes and add to cooker and bring up to 15 lb. pressure for six minutes.
5. Reduce pressure and remove bay leaf and place stew on a warmed serving dish. Arrange potatoes around side of dish. Serve with carrots and peas.

Roasted Forerib of Beef

Serves 6–8

25 g (1 oz.) lard
2.25 kg (5 lb.) joint forerib of beef
1–1.25 kg (2–3 lb.) potatoes
Salt
15 ml (1 tablespoon) plain flour
Pepper

1. Prepare oven (Gas Mark 4, 350°F).
2. Place lard in a roasting tin and melt in the oven.
3. Wipe the meat with a clean cloth and place in a roasting tin in centre of oven.
4. Peel potatoes and cut into pieces. Cook in boiling, salted water for five minutes. Drain and arrange potatoes around meat, basting them with the fat. Cook the meat and potatoes for about 2½ hours, basting with fat.
5. Lift meat out on to a hot dish, encircling the meat with the potatoes.
6. To make the gravy, strain the fat from the roasting tin. Stir in flour and 300 ml (½ pt.) of vegetable stock into juices in the tin. Bring to boil, stirring. Pour from a gravy boat.

Hotpot

Serves 6

700 g (1½ lb.) lean beef
3 onions
3 carrots
1 kg (2 lb.) potatoes
Salt and pepper
Stock

1. Remove fat from meat, then cut into pieces.

2. Skin and chop the onions and carrots into thin slices and peel and slice the potatoes.
3. Prepare oven (Gas Mark 3, 325°F).
4. Arrange the meat, onions, carrots and potatoes in layers in a casserole and season well. The top layer should be of potatoes. Three-quarters fill the casserole with stock, adding more later if the dish appears to be dry.
5. Cover and bake in oven for two hours, removing the cover 30 minutes before serving.

Farmhouse Pie—an ideal winter dish for hungry families

LAMB AND MUTTON

Scrag and Middle Cut

Middle neck chops used for stews and casseroles. Scrag end for soups and stews.

Best End Neck

Bone-in roast or cut into chops for braising, frying or grilling.

Loin

Roasting joint, but usually cut into loin and chumps chops for grilling or frying.

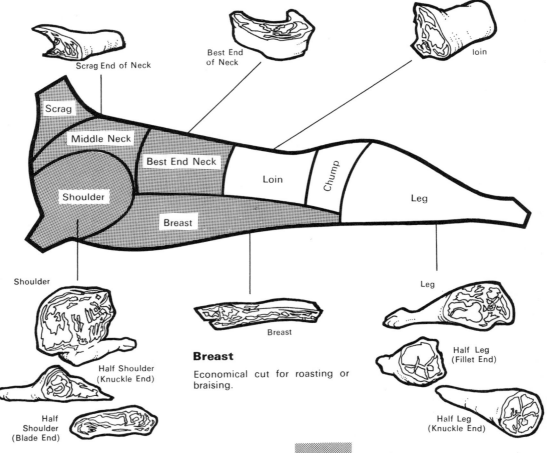

Scrag End of Neck

Best End of Neck

loin

Scrag

Middle Neck

Best End Neck

Loin

Chump

Leg

Shoulder

Breast

Shoulder

Leg

Breast

Half Shoulder (Knuckle End)

Half Leg (Fillet End)

Half Shoulder (Blade End)

Half Leg (Knuckle End)

Breast

Economical cut for roasting or braising.

Cheaper Cuts

Shoulder

Roasting joint either on or off the bone, often divided into small cuts. Blade end and knuckle end.

Leg

Roasting joint often divided into fillet and shank end.

Lamb and Mutton

The technical difference between mutton and lamb is primarily that of age—although there are other interpretations.

Lamb is generally taken to mean the meat of young sheep of either sex less than a year old. As far as the housewife is concerned the difference is in the eating quality.

Traditionally, lambs are born in the spring, but this varies with the climate —the first lambs being born in the south and then the rest are born progressively later towards the northern areas. Some 'out of season' lambs are produced for Christmas, for example, but these are very expensive and can be regarded as a special product. The first new season's lambs appear in the shops around Easter. Initially, prices are high but they usually fall as more lambs become available through the season.

Quality lamb can be identified by pale flesh with a light covering of fat. In young animals the flesh is light pink, while in mature animals it is light red. Colour of the lean does, however, vary according to source. Imported lamb is often a different colour due to the effect of freezing. Imported lamb has firm white fat, while English lamb available in spring and early summer has creamy-coloured fat. The lean meat of hill lamb is sometimes darker than that of lowland farms.

Bones should be pinkish with a blue tinge and the cartilage on the knuckle joints should be blue-white.

The size of lambs also varies considerably from 11 kg (25 lb.) in small hill lambs to 23 kg (50 lb.) or more in some of the heavier Down types. The average home produced lamb weighs 14–21 kg (30–45 lb.), but the New Zealand ones are slightly smaller.

Lamb marketing reaches a peak in October, when there are plenty of good lambs available at reasonable prices. Home produced lamb is in short supply from the end of the year onwards. At this time, supplies of new season's New Zealand lamb are newly arrived and at their best.

Carving Lamb

It's a good idea to 'rest' the meat on a warm serving dish for about 10 minutes before carving. Then when you're ready, cut slices about 5 mm ($\frac{1}{4}$ in.) thick.

Best End is cut between each rib and served as cutlets—though if you want thicker portions you can cut between alternate bones.

Leg is best tackled by first cutting out a 'wedge' down to the bone (see illustration) and then slicing down from both sides of the first cut. When the meat has been taken from that side, turn the joint over, remove bits of fat and carve horizontally along the leg.

Loin, roasted, should be cut in the same way as best end.

Shoulder is best started by carving a thick slice down to the bone (see illustration), continuing to slice from both sides of the first cut, with smaller slices over the blade bone. Finish carving the first side by cutting horizontally towards the shank, as shown. Then turn the joint over and carve horizontally. If the shoulder has been boned and rolled before cooking, simply carve downward slices.

How to Carve

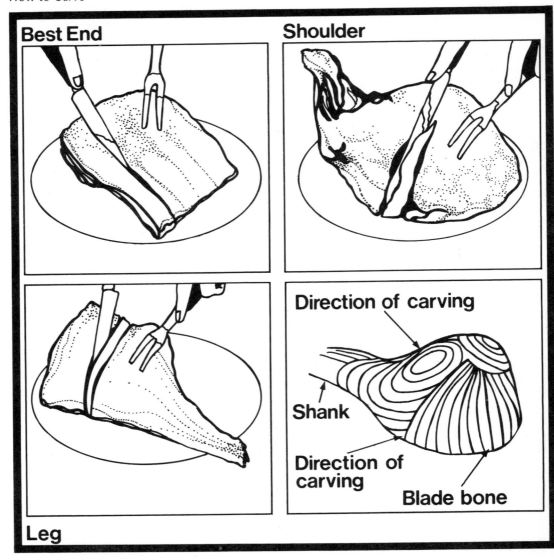

Best End

Shoulder

Direction of carving

Shank

Direction of carving

Blade bone

Leg

38

Ways of Serving Lamb

Barbecued Spare Ribs makes an unusual supper dish

Barbecued Spare Ribs

Serves 4

1 large breast of lamb, cut into ribs
600 ml (1 pt) boiling water
15 ml (1 tablespoon) vinegar

Sauce

15 ml (1 tablespoon) soy sauce
15 ml (1 tablespoon) clear honey
15 ml (1 tablespoon) plum jam (or
  any red jam)
$7\frac{1}{2}$ ml ($1\frac{1}{2}$ teaspoon) white vinegar
$2\frac{1}{2}$ ml ($\frac{1}{2}$ teaspoon) Worcester sauce
$2\frac{1}{2}$ ml ($\frac{1}{2}$ teaspoon) dry mustard
$2\frac{1}{2}$ ml ($\frac{1}{2}$ teaspoon) tomato ketchup
Squeeze of lemon juice

1. Remove any excess skin and fat from the ribs. Place in the boiling vinegar water. Simmer for 15 minutes, drain and place meat in a roasting tin.
2. Prepare oven (Gas Mark 4, 350°F). Mix all the sauce ingredients together and heat slowly in a saucepan for four minutes. Pour the sauce over the ribs.
3. Cook in oven for 30 minutes, then increase setting to Gas Mark 6 (400°F) for a further 20 minutes.
4. Serve with sauce.

Lamb Cobbler

Serves 4

1 kg (2 lb.) scrag end
2 medium onions
3 tomatoes
100 g (4 oz.) mushrooms
25 g (1 oz.) fat
25 g (1 oz.) flour
450 ml ($\frac{3}{4}$ pt.) stock
Salt and pepper

Scone Topping

225 g ($\frac{1}{2}$ lb.) flour
5 ml (1 teaspoon) bicarbonate of
  soda
10 ml (2 teaspoons) cream of tartar
2$\frac{1}{2}$ ml ($\frac{1}{2}$ teaspoon) mixed herbs
50 g (2 oz.) margarine
150 ml ($\frac{1}{4}$ pt.) milk

1. Cut and trim the lamb. Slice onions, tomatoes and mushrooms. Melt the fat and fry the onions and meat until lightly browned.
2. Prepare oven (Gas Mark 6, 400°F). Put meat, onions, tomatoes and mushrooms in layers into a casserole.
3. Stir the flour into the melted fat remaining in the pan and cook for a few minutes, then add the stock and seasoning. Bring to the boil and pour over the meat. Cook in oven for one hour.
4. While meat is cooking, make the scone topping. Mix all dry ingredients together and rub in the fat.
5. Just before the meat is cooked add the milk to the dry ingredients and mix to a soft dough. Roll out and cut into small scones. Place on top of the meat and cook for a further 20 minutes.

Hungarian Hotpot

Serves 4

1 kg (2 lb.) neck chops
15 ml (1 tablespoon) cooking oil
15 ml (1 tablespoon) paprika pepper
Salt and pepper
450 g (1 lb.) onions, roughly chopped
450 g (1 lb.) carrots, chopped, 25 mm
  (1 in.) pieces
300 ml ($\frac{1}{2}$ pt.) stock
1 small packet frozen peas
1 carton plain yoghurt (optional)
Parsley, chopped

1. Brown the neck chops on either side in the hot oil, then remove and drain.
2. Place the chops in a large saucepan and add the paprika, salt, pepper, onions, carrots and stock. Bring to the boil, cover and simmer for two hours. Add the peas for the last 15 minutes of cooking time.
3. Check seasoning. Serve topped with swirls of yoghurt and chopped parsley.

Lemon and Ginger Chops

Serves 4

4 chump chops

Marinade
60 ml (4 tablespoons) oil
Grated rind of one lemon
30 ml (2 tablespoons) lemon juice
15 ml (1 tablespoon) brown sugar
7$\frac{1}{2}$ ml (1$\frac{1}{2}$ teaspoon) ground ginger
Salt and pepper

1. Mix all the marinade ingredients together. Place the chops in a

shallow dish and pour the marinade over them. Leave for two to three hours, turning occasionally.
2. Remove the chops and place under a hot grill. Cook for 15 minutes, turning the chops occasionally and basting them with the marinade.
3. Garnish with sliced lemon.

Picnic Pie

Serves 4

350 g ($\frac{3}{4}$ lb.) shoulder, cubed. Buy
  half a shoulder about 575 g
  ($1\frac{1}{4}$ lb.)
1 large onion, chopped
300 ml ($\frac{1}{2}$ pt.) stock
45 ml (3 heaped tablespoons) sage
  and onion packet stuffing mix
Salt and pepper
50 g (2 oz.) mushrooms, sliced

Pastry

100 g (4 oz.) plain flour
50 g (2 oz.) margarine
5 ml (1 level teaspoon) salt
Water
1 egg, beaten (for glaze)

1. To make the filling, brown the cubes of lamb in a saucepan, without adding extra fat. Then add the onion and cook for 10 minutes on a gentle heat. Add the stock and simmer for a further 30 minutes. Add sage and onion stuffing and seasoning. Stir in sliced mushrooms then allow to cool.
2. While filling is cooling, prepare oven (Gas Mark 6, 400°F), then make the pastry by rubbing the fat into the sifted flour and salt to resemble breadcrumbs. Add sufficient water to form a pliable dough. Roll out two-thirds of dough and line a 1 lb. tin. Reserve remaining dough to form a lid for the pie.
3. Once filling has cooled, pack it into the prepared case. Top with reserved pastry, using a small quantity to form a decorative 'rose'. Brush with beaten egg to glaze.
4. Bake for 30–35 minutes. Cool before removing from tin. Serve hot or cold.

Noisettes of Lamb Garni

Serves 4

700 g ($1\frac{1}{2}$ lb.) best end neck
4 large firm tomatoes
700 g ($1\frac{1}{2}$ lb.) hot mashed potatoes
1 can peas or cooked peas

1. Prepare oven (Gas Mark 5, 375°F). Divide the lamb into cutlets and remove the bone. Cut the end around the edge of the cutlet and secure with a small skewer.
2. Cut the tomatoes in half and scoop out the centres, keeping the tomato pulp on one side to use in the gravy.
3. Pipe or spread a layer of potato down the centre of an ovenproof dish, surround with tomato shells and place dish in oven for about 15 minutes.
4. Grill or fry the noisettes of lamb for about six to eight minutes on each side, then arrange on potato.
5. Meanwhile heat the peas, then drain. Use the liquid for the gravy, thickening with flour in the usual way. Add dripping from cooking noisettes and the tomato pulp. Pile the peas into the tomato shells and serve.

Cinnamon Pot Roast of Lamb

Serves 4

$\frac{1}{2}$ leg of lamb
1 clove garlic
15 ml (1 tablespoon) flour
5 ml (1 teaspoon) cinnamon
Salt and pepper
15 ml (1 tablespoon) oil
225 g ($\frac{1}{2}$ lb.) carrots
225 g ($\frac{1}{2}$ lb.) small onions
1 stick of celery
900 ml ($1\frac{1}{2}$ pt.) stock or water

Stuffing Mix

1 small onion
15 ml (1 tablespoon) oil
30 ml (2 tablespoons) breadcrumbs
100 g (4 oz.) pork sausagemeat
5 ml (1 teaspoon) rosemary
Salt and pepper
1 egg yolk

1. Remove the bone from the lamb (or ask your butcher to do this).
2. Make stuffing. Chop the onion and fry in the oil for a few minutes, then add the breadcrumbs, sausagemeat, rosemary and seasoning. Bind together with the egg yolk. Spread the stuffing on the meat, then roll up and tie securely with string. Insert slivers of garlic under the skin.
3. Mix together the flour, cinnamon, pepper and salt and rub on to the joint. Heat the oil in a *large* pan and brown the joint on all sides.
4. Remove the joint, slice vegetables and gently fry in the hot oil.
5. Place the joint on top of the vegetables, add stock or water, cover and cook over a moderate heat for about 2–$2\frac{1}{2}$ hours. Move the joint

occasionally to prevent sticking, adding more liquid if necessary.

Stuffed Shoulder

Serves 4

1 boned shoulder of lamb
225 g (8 oz.) sausagemeat
30 ml (2 tablespoons) sage and
 onion packet stuffing mix
$2\frac{1}{2}$ ml ($\frac{1}{2}$ teaspoon) mixed herbs
15 ml (1 tablespoon) chutney
Salt and pepper

1. Clean and prepare shoulder. Prepare oven (Gas Mark 4, 350°F).
2. Mix together the sausagemeat, stuffing mix and seasonings and spread on shoulder. Roll up the meat and tie securely.
3. Roast in oven, allowing 35 minutes per lb. plus 35 minutes.
4. Serve with vegetables in season.

Breadcrumbed Breast

Serves 4

1 breast of lamb
600 ml (1 pt.) stock
1 egg, beaten
Breadcrumbs
Oil for frying
Lemon, sliced

1. Boil breast in stock until tender. Remove bones and excess fat, then cut into small pieces.
2. Coat with egg and breadcrumbs and fry in hot oil until golden brown.
3. Garnish with vegetables and lemon slices.

Gourmet Roast Shoulder

Serves 6

1 shoulder of lamb
1 clove of garlic
Cooking oil
Salt and pepper
30 ml (2 tablespoons) flour
25 g (1 oz.) dripping or lard
150 ml ($\frac{1}{4}$ pt.) orange juice
45 ml (3 tablespoons) demerara sugar

1. Prepare oven (Gas Mark 4, 350°F). Wipe the joint with a damp cloth. Rub the skin over with a cut clove of garlic, then make small incisions in the skin of the joint and insert slivers of garlic. Brush the skin over with oil, then dust with seasoned flour.
2. Place the joint in a roasting tin with the dripping or lard and roast in oven, allowing 25–30 minutes for each pound, plus 30 minutes.
3. When half cooked sprinkle the meat with half the orange juice and repeat 10 minutes later. About 10 minutes before the end of the cooking time, sprinkle the meat with the sugar.

Crusty Coated Lamb

Serves 4–6

1 leg of lamb
Cooking oil
45 ml (3 tablespoons) fresh
  breadcrumbs
15 ml (1 tablespoon) chopped parsley
1 clove garlic
Salt and pepper

1. Prepare oven (Gas Mark 4, 350°F).
2. Brush surface of leg with a little cooking oil and place in a roasting tin. Mix together the breadcrumbs, parsley, finely crushed garlic and seasoning. Sprinkle the mixture on top of the joint.
3. Roast in oven, allowing 30 minutes for each pound. Baste once towards the end of cooking time.

Apricot Lamb

Serves 4

4 loin chops
1 medium-sized tin of apricot halves
15 ml (1 tablespoon) cooking oil
15 ml (1 tablespoon) butter
5 ml (1 teaspoon) salt
Pinch of pepper
30 ml (2 tablespoons) dried milk
  powder
15 ml (1 tablespoon) onion soup
  powder
150 ml ($\frac{1}{4}$ pt.) dry white wine
30 ml (2 tablespoons) double cream
Pinch cayenne pepper

1. Place chops on a flat dish, with apricot halves on top and leave for two to three hours.
2. Heat oil and butter in a frying pan. Lift off apricots, sprinkle chops with salt and pepper and rub in the mixture of milk and onion soup powders.
3. Fry gently for about 15 minutes each side, until crisp and golden. Remove and keep hot.
4. Pour off excess fat, then gently fry apricots for about $1\frac{1}{2}$ minutes each side and arrange around the chops.
5. Add the wine to the pan and bring to the boil. Reduce the heat, stir in cream and add the cayenne pepper.
6. To serve, spoon the sauce over the apricots and garnish if required.

PORK

Shoulder

Usually divided into blade and spare rib. Blade bone is a tasty joint. Spare rib is a tasty roasting joint, but often divided into chops for braising, frying or grilling.

Loin

Roasting joint on the bone. Often cut into chops for grilling or frying.

Leg

Roasting joint often divided into fillet and knuckle end.

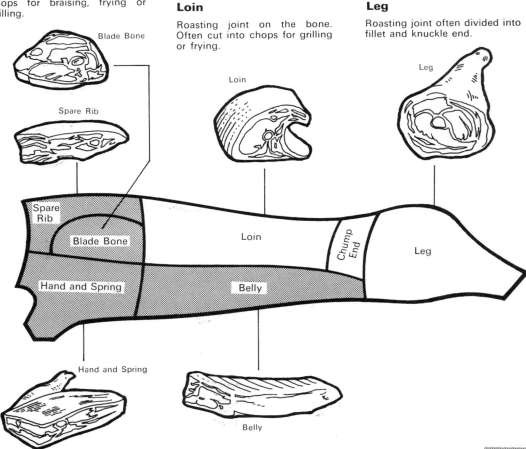

Blade Bone

Spare Rib

Loin

Leg

Spare Rib

Blade Bone

Loin

Chump End

Leg

Hand and Spring

Belly

Hand and Spring

Belly

Hand and Spring

The hand is best boned and rolled before roasting. The shank is used for stews and casseroles.

Belly

Economical roasting joint, usually stuffed and rolled. Belly slices for braising or frying.

Cheaper Cuts

Pork

Shopping for Pork

Pork is a distinctive and versatile meat and one to suit all purses. Because, too, the older pigs are used to make bacon, the pork that finds its way into the butcher's shop is almost always from young, tender animals.

Nearly all the pork consumed in the British Isles is home produced throughout the year and the pigs are slaughtered young to meet the increasing demand for lean meat. Larger pigs and breeding stock which are older and fatter are mainly used in meat processing.

As with any meat, though, it's important to look for flesh of good quality, and freshness is all-important. Flesh should be pale, pinkish in colour, 'fine grained', smooth and firm (not excessively wet or exuding moisture), with firm milky-white fat. Avoid fat that is grey or oily. The bones should be pinkish not yellowish. Rind or skin should be thin, pliable, smooth and free of hair. Avoid buying pork if the flesh has a reddish tinge, it's probably from an older animal; brownish, coarse flesh suggests either staleness or an ageing animal. Avoid pork that is greyish in colour.

Small black spots that may occasionally be found in the fat of some pork are, however, quite harmless. They are simply pigmentation spots from the skin of some types of pigs.

Pork often has a good proportion of fat, but don't be put off by this—it need not be wasted. Rendered down, the strained fat can be used for frying or making pastry.

Despite the old wives' tale that it should only be eaten when there's an 'r' in the month (in other words, not the summer months), pork can be enjoyed all the year round. The practice of avoiding pork in the hot months may have had some justification in the days before cold storage, but fortunately we can now overcome these difficulties. There is, however, one lesson to be learned from this—pork does not keep as well as other meats in a hot atmosphere—so keep it cool and covered (see p. 12).

Great care must be taken in storing pork in the freezer because, of all the meats, it is the most difficult to freeze and store successfully. Problems of rancidity may be encountered after two months or even less at frozen temperatures.

Because there is a slightly higher risk of harmful micro-organisms in pork than other meats, it's particularly important to make sure it is well cooked. Always overcook pork rather than undercook it.

Most pork joints can be roasted, boiled and salted, which provides variety. Selected cuts such as legs and loins (for chops) which have the

Pork and Bean Casserole—a new bean dish for the children

greatest demand tend to be expensive. The average porker pig will weigh between 41 kg (90 lb.) and 50 kg (110 lb.) and is normally cut with the bone, but butchers will de-bone and prepare cuts on demand. To produce crackling, the rind must be well 'scored' before cooking.

Carving

Knuckle End of Leg. An easy joint to carve. It is often best to remove crackling first, but it can be left on. Cut 5 mm ($\frac{1}{4}$ in.) slices on the thick side of the joint, carving down to the bones at a slight angle. Serve with a little crackling.

Fillet End of Leg. Again, carving is easier if the crackling is removed first. Place joint flat and carve a few 5 mm ($\frac{1}{4}$ in.) slices from the fat edge towards the base, then turn joint round and cut in from other side. Continue like this, trying to keep both sides level. Serve some crackling with each portion.

Belly. Lay with flat, fat side to the top and cut downwards across the grain of the meat in 5 mm ($\frac{1}{4}$ in.) slices. Rolled belly is cut downwards across the grain of the meat in 5 mm ($\frac{1}{4}$ in.) slices.

Hand and Spring. This can be a difficult joint to carve well. Carve from either side of the bone, across the grain of the meat.

Loin. Set the joint with the backbone downwards and cut downwards through the rib bones to divide into chops. Boned, rolled, loin should be carved in fairly thick slices.

Spare Rib. Carving is simply achieved by cutting down between the bones to form chops.

Blade. The crackling can be removed first to make carving easier, or it can be left on. Slice through to the bone (slices will be shorter in the centre because of the shape of the bone), then turn over and slice at an oblique angle to get the largest pieces possible.

Ways of Serving Pork

Stuffed Blade

Serves 4

1 blade of pork (about 1.5 kg (3 lb.)
  with bone)
1 small apple
1 × 439 g (15½ oz.) tin apricot halves
1 × 212 g (7½ oz.) tin pineapple rings
1 small onion
50 g (2 oz.) margarine
25 g (1 oz.) fresh breadcrumbs
5 ml (1 teaspoon) dried rosemary,
  crushed
Salt
Cooking oil
1 chicken stock cube
Boiling water
12½ ml (2½ teaspoons) cornflour

1. Prepare oven (Gas Mark 5, 375°F).
2. Remove bone (the butcher will do this for you if you ask him). Score skin of pork finely with a sharp knife (the butcher may have done this for you). Rub skin with salt.
3. Peel, core and cut apple into ¼ in. dice. Open apricot and pineapple tins. Reserve four apricot halves and two pineapple rings for garnish; chop remainder into roughly ¼ in. pieces.
4. Reserve apricot syrup. Peel and chop onion.
5. Melt margarine in a small saucepan and add onion. Fry for about four minutes.
6. Mix together apple, apricot, pineapple and onion. Add breadcrumbs and rosemary. Season with salt.
7. Place stuffing in bone cavity and firm the joint into shape, securing with skewers.
8. Brush joint with cooking oil and sprinkle with salt.
9. Cook in centre of oven for about 1¾ hours, or until the joint is ready.
10. Place cooked joint on a warmed serving dish and keep warm. Strain most of fat from the roasting tin and reserve.
11. Dissolve chicken stock cube in boiling water.
12. Blend cornflour with reserved apricot syrup in a saucepan. Stir in the meat juices, then add the chicken stock. Bring to boil, stirring continuously and boil for one minute. Strain into a warmed serving dish or gravy boat.
13. Garnish joint on serving dish with reserved apricots and pineapple. Chop apricot into small pieces, arrange rings one at each end of the joint and fill with chopped apricot.
14. Serve with roast potatoes and a green vegetable.

Stuffed Pig's Feet

Serves 4

4 pig's feet
30 ml (2 tablespoons) chopped and
   cooked onion
15 ml (1 tablespoon) white
   breadcrumbs
5 ml (1 teaspoon) powdered sage
Salt and pepper
15 ml (1 tablespoon) melted butter
1 egg
Breadcrumbs for coating
Lard or fat for frying

1. Put feet in saucepan and cover with salted water. Boil gently for two hours.
2. Mix onion, breadcrumbs, sage and seasoning. Bind with melted butter.
3. Split the feet, remove the bones and press the stuffing in the cavities. Press halves together again, tie with string or tape and press between boards or two dishes with weights on top. Leave to go cold.
4. When cold, slice into thin rounds, roll in the egg and breadcrumbs, then fry gently until golden brown. Garnish with parsley.

Stuffed Pigs' Ears

Serves 4

8 pigs' ears
Stock (or water)
Lard or cooking fat
Forcemeat stuffing

1. Wash ears and soak overnight.
2. Simmer in stock or water for 1½ hours.
3. Remove from stock (reserve stock).
4. Lift skin of upper side of ears and insert the forcemeat stuffing and secure the openings.
5. Prepare oven (Gas Mark 4, 350°F). Fry in fat until lightly browned.
6. Place in a shallow ovenproof dish, add reserved stock, cover and cook for about one hour.
7. Drain well and serve with a brown sauce.

Pork and Bean Casserole

Serves 4–6

225 g (8 oz.) red kidney or haricot
   beans
1 kg (2 lb.) blade or shoulder
25 g (1 oz.) seasoned flour
30 ml (2 tablespoons) oil
2 onions
500 g (1 lb.) carrots
1 green pepper
400 ml (¾ pt.) stock
Salt and pepper

1. Soak beans overnight, in water containing a pinch of bicarbonate of soda.
2. Prepare oven (Gas Mark 3, 325°F). Skin and dice the meat, then toss in seasoned flour.
3. Heat oil and fry meat until lightly browned.
4. Peel and slice onions and carrots. De-seed and slice green pepper. Place meat, onions, carrots, green pepper and stock into casserole and season, mixing well.
5. Cover casserole tightly and place in oven for three hours.
6. Add beans for last 30 minutes. Serve with jacket potatoes.

Pork and Bacon Loaf

Serves 6–8

450 g (1 lb.) belly pork
225 g (8 oz.) unsmoked back bacon
225 g (8 oz.) white breadcrumbs
1 onion
5 ml (1 teaspoon) dry mustard
2½ ml (½ teaspoon) mixed herbs
Salt and pepper
1 egg
120 ml (8 tablespoons) cider

1. Prepare oven (Gas Mark 4, 350°F). Mince pork and bacon. Peel and chop onion.
2. Place all dry ingredients in a mixing bowl, then add beaten egg and cider to bind.
3. Turn into a well-buttered 2 lb. loaf tin and cover with greased paper. Bake for 1½ hours.
4. When cooked, turn out of tin. Serve sliced, hot or cold.

Pig's Cheek in Breadcrumbs

Serves 3–4

1 pig's cheek
Browned breadcrumbs

1. Wash cheek well, changing water several times.
2. Cover meat with water and bring to boil, then simmer for about 2½ hours.
3. Prepare oven (Gas Mark 4, 350°F). Remove the cheek from the water and take off the skin. Cover with breadcrumbs, then bake for about half hour.
4. Serve hot or cold.
Note: The baking can be omitted if preferred.

Pot Roasted Hand of Pork with Rice

Serves 6–8

Mixed vegetables (including onion)
25 g (1 oz.) lard
1 chicken stock cube or stock
400 ml (¾ pt.) boiling water
Salt and pepper
1 bay leaf
1 hand of pork, about 2 kg (4½ lb.)
50 g (2 oz.) long-grain rice

1. Prepare and slice vegetables.
2. Melt lard in a large pan. Fry vegetables for five minutes.
3. Prepare chicken stock cube with boiling water (or use stock) and add to vegetables. Bring to boil. Add salt and pepper and bay leaf.
4. Place joint in saucepan and cover with lid. Bring back to boil and simmer for two hours, or until ready.
5. Remove meat and place on a warmed serving dish. Keep warm.
6. Remove bay leaf and add washed rice to saucepan and cook slowly, covered, for about 10 minutes, then uncover and cook until rice is tender (test by pressing between thumb and finger). If necessary, strain any excess liquor and wash rice under running hot water to prevent grains from sticking together.
7. Remove knuckle bone and skin from pork and arrange the vegetables and rice mixture around the joint.

BACON

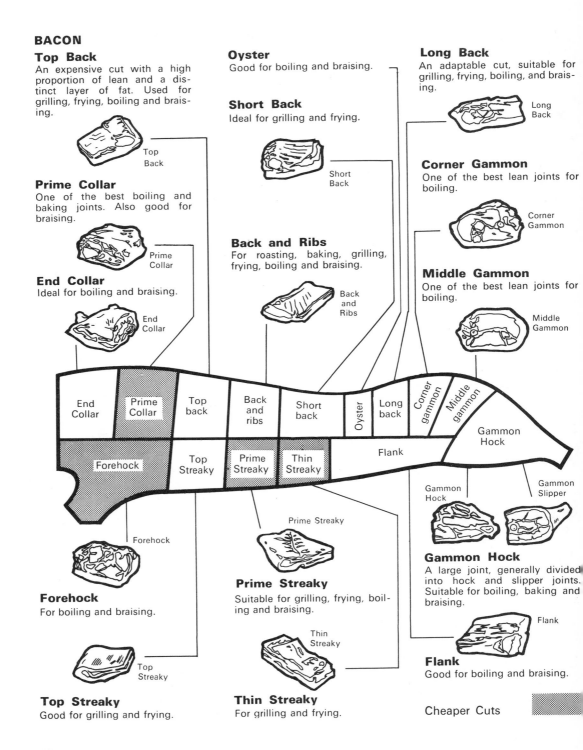

Top Back
An expensive cut with a high proportion of lean and a distinct layer of fat. Used for grilling, frying, boiling and braising.

Prime Collar
One of the best boiling and baking joints. Also good for braising.

End Collar
Ideal for boiling and braising.

Oyster
Good for boiling and braising.

Short Back
Ideal for grilling and frying.

Back and Ribs
For roasting, baking, grilling, frying, boiling and braising.

Long Back
An adaptable cut, suitable for grilling, frying, boiling, and braising.

Corner Gammon
One of the best lean joints for boiling.

Middle Gammon
One of the best lean joints for boiling.

Forehock
For boiling and braising.

Prime Streaky
Suitable for grilling, frying, boiling and braising.

Gammon Hock
A large joint, generally divided into hock and slipper joints. Suitable for boiling, baking and braising.

Flank
Good for boiling and braising.

Top Streaky
Good for grilling and frying.

Thin Streaky
For grilling and frying.

Cheaper Cuts

50

Bacon and Ham

The difference between bacon and ham is one of curing. Meat for bacon or gammon is salted down for about three weeks. At this stage the rind is pale coloured, the flesh pink, and the bacon is known as 'green'.

If the 'green' bacon is then smoked it becomes a golden brown and the flesh turns darker—and the result is smoked bacon.

Gammon is hind leg smoked separately after salting. Ham is cut off the bone before salting and curing in one of several ways.

Vacuum-packed bacon for grilling and frying is usually of high quality, though often expensive. It has a comparatively long life and the packs are date-stamped to make sure the bacon is enjoyed in a prime condition.

Boil-in-the-bag bacon joints are specially sealed and usually have instructions on the bag. As the joints are mild cured they can be cooked in the bag, which helps to keep the joint in good shape, as well as retaining the natural meat juices.

Fresh bacon has a pleasant smell; the lean areas should be pink, the fat white and firm. A good proportion of fat to lean is necessary for flavour and texture.

The colour of the rind will depend on how the bacon has been treated—unsmoked will be pale cream, smoked a light or dark golden colour.

Club Streaky—an unusual and attractive way of serving bacon

Ways of Serving Bacon and Ham

Cider Bacon with Apple Sauce is an exciting dish

Cider Bacon with Apple Sauce

Serves 6–8

1 kg (2½ lb.) collar joint
300 ml (½ pt.) cider
1 onion
1 carrot
Bay leaf
Bouquet garni
Peppercorns
Toasted breadcrumbs

Apple Sauce

450 g (1 lb.) cooking apples
50 g (2 oz.) raisins
150 ml (¼ pt.) stock from bacon joint

1. Bring bacon to boil in plain water. Drain and place joint in the cider and enough fresh water to cover. Add prepared vegetables and seasoning.
2. Bring back to boil, reduce heat and simmer gently, allowing 20 minutes for each pound and 20 minutes over. Keep the lid on the saucepan and check occasionally to make sure there is enough water in the pan.
3. When cooked, drain joint, reserving 150 ml (¼ pt.) stock for the sauce. Remove rind and coat top of joint with toasted breadcrumbs.
4. Slice and stew the apples and raisins with the bacon stock to make a thick apple sauce, adding sugar to taste.

5. Serve joint and sauce hot with mashed potatoes and spring cabbage, or cold with salad.

Club Streaky

Serves 10–12

2 kg (4 lb.) streaky bacon
Bay leaves

Stuffing

100 g (4 oz.) dried apricots
100 g (4 oz.) breadcrumbs
1 stick of celery, chopped
15 ml (1 tablespoon) chopped parsley
Salt and pepper
1 egg

1. Divide bacon in two and bring pieces to the boil in plenty of cold water, adding three or four bay leaves. Drain, cut off the rind.
2. Soak apricots for 15 minutes in boiling water; reserve two for decoration and chop remainder.
3. Prepare oven (Gas Mark 4, 350°F). Mix stuffing ingredients and spread mixture on rib side of one half of bacon. Cover with other half, score top fat. Press pieces together, tie and wrap in foil. Bake in oven, allowing 30 minutes for each pound. Open foil for final 15 minutes to brown top. Sprinkle on a little brown sugar if a glazed finish is required.
4. Decorate with the reserved apricots and fresh bay leaves if available. Serve sliced thinly when cold.

Bacon and Bean Bake

Serves 4

800 g (1¾ lb.) forehock joint
25 g (1 oz.) butter
1 onion
100 g (4 oz.) carrots
30 ml (2 tablespoons) tomato purée
1 × 141 g (5 oz.) tin baked beans
Pepper

1. Place bacon in cold water and bring to the boil. Drain, cover with fresh cold water and bring to boil again. Reduce heat and simmer for 20 minutes.
2. Melt the butter, add the sliced onion and carrots and cook gently for about five minutes. Stir in the flour, gradually add the water, bring to boil, simmer for two minutes until thickened. Stir in tomato purée and beans. Add a little pepper.
3. Prepare oven (Gas Mark 4, 350°F).
4. Drain joint and remove rind. Place joint in casserole. Pour over sauce. Cover and cook in oven for 1¼ hours.

Fried Bacon Chops

Serves 3

3 × 100 g (4 oz.) bacon chops
Fat, for frying
Tomatoes
Mushrooms

1. Remove rind from the chops and snip the fat at intervals. Fry the chops gently, adding a little extra fat to the pan if necessary. Allow five minutes for each side.
2. Serve with fried mushrooms and tomatoes.

Danish Hash

Serves 3-4

450 g (1 lb.) potatoes
2 large onions
350 g (12 oz.) bacon
75 g (3 oz.) butter
Salt and pepper

1. Peel and dice potatoes into 1 cm ($\frac{1}{2}$ in.) pieces. Place in pan of cold salted water, bring to boil and cook gently for five minutes, until just tender.
2. Peel and slice the onions.
3. Melt the butter and fry the bacon quickly, turning frequently until brown all over (about five minutes). Remove with a slotted spoon and keep hot.
4. Add the onions and cook until soft. Add the potatoes and cook quickly for about three minutes to brown. Return the meat to the pan and heat through gently.
5. Season with salt and pepper.
6. Serve with fried eggs.

Bacon Stewpot

Serves 4

700 g (1$\frac{1}{2}$ lb.) bacon slipper joint or
  collar, unsmoked
225 g (8 oz.) leeks
1 onion, chopped
40 g (1$\frac{1}{2}$ oz.) butter
30 ml (2 tablespoons) flour
450 ml ($\frac{3}{4}$ pt.) stock
100 g (4 oz.) carrots
Pepper
212 g (7$\frac{1}{2}$ oz.) can butter beans
Parsley

1. Remove rind and any excess fat from the bacon. Cut the meat into 2 cm ($\frac{3}{4}$ in.) diced pieces. Place in cold water and bring slowly to the boil. Drain the pieces. Prepare leeks and cook in the butter with the onions until soft.
2. Stir in flour, gradually adding stock and bring to the boil to thicken. Add carrots peeled and sliced, the bacon and some pepper. Cover and cook gently for 1$\frac{1}{4}$ hours.
3. Add the drained butter beans and chopped parsley about 10 minutes before serving.

Bacon Omelette

Serves 3-4

225 g (8 oz.) back rashers
15 ml (1 tablespoon) flour
90 ml (6 tablespoons) milk
4 eggs
Salt and pepper
12 g ($\frac{1}{2}$ oz.) butter

Garnish

Parsley or chives
Tomato

1. Remove the rinds from the bacon rashers. Place the rashers on the grill pan and cook until golden brown and crisp (about three to four minutes).
2. Meanwhile blend the flour and milk. Beat in the eggs and season.
3. Melt butter in a frying pan, and heat until just turning brown. Pour in the egg mixture and cook over a fairly high heat until set, lifting the edges occasionally. When cooked through, about five to six minutes, place the hot bacon rashers on top.

4. Garnish with chopped chives or parsley and wedges of tomato. Serve straight from the pan.

Bacon and Potato Pie

Serves 4

225 g (8 oz.) rindless back bacon
Large packet of instant mashed potato
2 large onions
50 g (2 oz.) butter or lard
Parsley or tomato for garnish

1. Fry the bacon rashers gently and prepare the mashed potatoes. Peel and slice the onions. Remove the bacon.
2. Fry the onions in the bacon fat until golden brown, adding a little butter or lard if necessary.
3. Pile the mashed potato into the centre of a hot dish. Arrange the rashers of bacon on the potatoes and place the cooked onions on top. Garnish with chopped parsley or tomato slices.

Steaks with Redcurrant Sauce

Serves 2

2 × 175 g (6 oz.) gammon steaks
Butter
1 eating apple
30 ml (2 tablespoons) redcurrant jelly
5 ml (1 teaspoon) wine vinegar
5 ml (1 teaspoon) brown sugar

1. Snip the rind off the steaks to prevent curling during the cooking. Brush one side with melted butter and cook under fairly hot grill for five minutes. Turn the steaks, brush with butter.
2. Cut apple in four slices, remove core and brush with butter. Grill steaks

and apple for a further five minutes, turning the apples once. Keep hot.
3. Retain liquid in grill pan, add remaining ingredients, stir and melt jelly over a medium heat until blended and slightly syrupy. Arrange the gammon steaks on a serving dish with two apple slices on each. Spoon the sauce over each and decorate with a sprig of parsley.

Ham and Rice Salad

Serves 4

100 g (4 oz.) long-grained rice
2 eggs
Pinch each salt, pepper, dry mustard, castor sugar
45 ml (3 tablespoons) oil
22 ml (1½ tablespoons) white vinegar
225 g (8 oz.) ham, cooked and sliced 1 cm (½ in.) thick
100 g (4 oz.) cucumber
Lettuce
Chives

1. Cook the rice in boiling, salted, water until tender, about 12–15 minutes. Drain, rinse and cool.
2. Hard boil the eggs for 12 minutes, drain and cool under cold water.
3. Place the seasonings in a mixing bowl with the castor sugar. Blend in the oil and gradually beat in the vinegar. Stir in the cooled rice.
4. Cut the ham into thin strips. Cut the cucumbers into thin slices. Add these to the rice, mix well.
5. Arrange lettuce leaves around a serving dish. Pile the rice and ham mixture in the centre. Peel the eggs, cut into quarters and arrange between the lettuce.
6. Sprinkle with chopped chives.

Poultry and Game

The frozen chicken has had a tremendous impact on our meat-eating habits—and has brought home the importance of poultry in our menus. But there is a lot more to be enjoyed than just a ready-prepared chicken.

Poultry are domestic birds specially bred for the table and include chicken, duck, goose, guinea fowl and turkey.

Chicken. The flavour depends on its age. In a young bird the tip of the breastbone is soft and flexible and the feet are smooth with small scales. As the bird becomes older the breastbone is harder and its flesh darker and drier.

The length of time a bird is left after killing and before 'drawing' influences the flavour. The longer it is left, the stronger the flavour.

Chickens are available as fresh or frozen throughout the year from 700 g (1¼ lb.) up to 2.75 kg (6 lb.) (untrussed weight) and are very good value.

Capon is a young castrated cock bird, specially bred to give a high proportion of flesh of good flavour. Available from 2 kg (5 lb.) to 4.5 kg (10 lb.), although larger birds are available at special times.

Duck can be purchased all year in a weight range of 2 kg (4 lb.) to 2.75 kg (6 lb.), but are best from August to December. The breast must be plump and the bird's underbill soft enough to bend. The duck contains a fair amount of fat and is best roasted. There is a limited amount of meat on a duck carcass and a 2.75 kg (6 lb.) bird will only serve four people. Very heavy duck should be avoided as the extra weight will be almost entirely fat.

Ducklings are small duck weighing 1.5 kg (3½ lb.) to 2 kg (4 lb.) and are at their best from April to July.

Goose should be plump and have soft yellow feet. This is a fatty bird which has a slight 'gamey' flavour. The average weight is between 2.75–5.5 kg (6–12 lb.). Goose is available frozen all year, but fresh birds are best from October to February. With declining demand, supplies of geese are becoming more difficult to find.

Turkeys are obtainable as fresh or frozen, either whole or in joints and also boned and rolled. They have a weight range from 2.75–18 kg (6–40 lb.), the average being 4.5–6.25 kg (10–14 lb.). Hens are preferred for the smaller weights because they are plumper with smaller bones. They are usually dearer than the larger cock birds. Prices for frozen birds remain fairly stable throughout the year, but the price of fresh birds increases with demand at Christmas time.

Guinea Fowl were originally game birds but are now bred for the table. They are best hung a few days. The flesh is creamy white, slightly resembling that of pheasant. They are suitable for roasting, braising or casseroling. They are marketed all year and are said to be at their best from February to April.

Toscana Chicken

Ways of Serving Poultry

Chicken Casserole

Serves 4

450 g (1 lb.) tomatoes
100 g (4 oz.) streaky bacon
2 large onions
100 g (4 oz.) mushrooms
50 g (2 oz.) plain flour
Salt
4 chicken leg joints
50 g (2 oz.) butter
300 ml ($\frac{1}{2}$ pt.) water
5 ml (1 teaspoon) castor sugar

1. Prepare oven (Gas Mark 5, 375°F). Immerse tomatoes in boiling water for one minute, drain and peel.
2. Bone bacon, remove rind and slice into 1 cm ($\frac{1}{2}$ in.) strips. Peel onions and slice in rings. Wash mushrooms and cut into quarters.
3. Dust chicken legs with flour and salt. Melt butter in a large frying pan and fry chicken joints until golden brown.
4. Place the joints in a $3\frac{1}{2}$ pint casserole, adding the tomatoes. Place the onions, bacon and mushrooms in frying pan and fry for two minutes. Stir in remaining flour together with water and castor sugar. Bring to boil and pour over chicken. Cover and place in centre of oven for one hour.

Toscana Chicken

Serves 4–6

1.5 kg (3 lb.) chicken
Water to cover
1 bay leaf
6 pepper corns
1 cucumber
15 ml (1 tablespoon) chopped parsley
25 g (1 oz.) butter
Seasoning
100 g (4 oz.) button mushrooms
25 g (1 oz.) butter
25 g (1 oz.) flour
600 ml (1 pt.) stock
2 lemons
50 ml ($\frac{1}{8}$ pt.) cream

1. Poach the chicken gently in the water with the bay leaf and pepper-corns until tender (about 1–$1\frac{1}{2}$ hours). Peel the cucumber and cut into strips about $2\frac{1}{2}$ cm (1 in.) long and toss in butter until tender. Then add the parsley and season to taste.
2. Toss the halved mushrooms in butter until tender.
3. Melt the butter, stir in the flour and cook until the mixture is a nut brown colour. Blend in the stock and thicken over a moderate heat.
4. Peel the rind off the lemons and cut into needle shreds. Squeeze the

juice from the whole lemons. Add the lemon juice to the sauce.

5. Put the chicken on a serving dish and surround with the cucumber and mushrooms. Just before serving add the cream to the sauce and spoon over the chicken. Sprinkle the shreds of lemon peel down the centre of the bird and serve.

Duck Casserole

Serves 3–4

175 g (6 oz.) chestnuts
3 onions
100 g (4 oz.) mushrooms
25 g (1 oz.) flour
50 g (2 oz.) butter
300 ml ($\frac{1}{2}$ pt.) stock
Pinch dried sage
Salt and pepper
1 duck

1. Split chestnuts and boil for eight minutes, immediately removing the skins.
2. Skin and slice onions and lightly fry in butter, then place in casserole.
3. Clean and slice mushrooms and add to casserole. Stir flour into frying pan juices and cook for three minutes. Add the stock and bring to boil, cooking until slightly thickened. Add sage and seasoning.
4. Prepare oven (Gas Mark 3, 325°F).
5. Clean and prepare duck and place in casserole, breast side up. Add the peeled chestnuts and cover with lid or foil. Cook in centre of oven for about $2\frac{1}{2}$ hours. To brown the breast remove lid and increase oven temperature to Gas Mark 6 (400°F) for 15 minutes.

Orange Roast Duck

Serves 4

1 large duck
Fat for basting
1 large orange
15 ml (1 tablespoon) red wine

1. Prepare oven (Gas Mark 5, 375°F). Pluck and truss the duck, then roast for 1–1$\frac{1}{2}$ hours until tender. Use fat to baste duck.
2. Meanwhile, stand the orange in boiling water for four minutes, remove skin and cut orange into segments, soaking them in wine. Heat orange segments moderately.
3. Serve with orange segments as a garnish.

Slimmer's Chicken

Serves 4

1.5 kg (3 lb.) chicken
1 carton cottage cheese
5 ml (1 teaspoon) chopped parsley
5 ml (1 teaspoon) chopped mixed herbs
Salt
25 g (1 oz.) butter

1. Thaw the chicken, if frozen.
2. Prepare oven (Gas Mark 4, 350°F).
3. Combine the cottage cheese with the herbs and seasoning (don't use too much salt) until they are well blended. Stuff the chicken with the herb and cheese mixture.
4. Place a knob of butter on the chicken and then roast in oven for 1–1$\frac{1}{2}$ hours, or until golden and tender.
5. Serve hot with a coleslaw salad.

Offal

Offal is often neglected, yet it can provide some real table delicacies—in some cases very cheaply. If you don't regularly use offal, it's worth experimenting—there is a whole variety of tastes to be explored.

Brains are sold in sets—one set of lamb's brains usually being enough for one person. A set of calve's brains will be enough for two. Calve's brains are considered best, but be sure they are fresh.

Feet or Trotters. Calve's or pig's feet are used for brawn and, because of their high gelatine content, to set moulds.

Hearts are somewhat neglected, but lamb's and pig's hearts are good stuffed and roasted, or braised. Ox heart is inclined to be tough and needs to be cooked slowly in a casserole.

One lamb's or pig's heart is enough for one person, a calve's heart should serve two, an ox heart about four.

Wash hearts well in cold water, trim away fat and waste, then snip the wall dividing the centre. Soak for an hour in clean salted water, then rinse and drain.

Kidneys can be used in many ways— as savoury dishes in themselves, served on toast, grilled with bacon, made into a rich stew, or as an ingredient in casseroles, pies or puddings.

Lamb's kidneys are ideal for grills, sautés and braises. Pig's kidneys have a stronger flavour and should be soaked in milk for about half an hour before cooking. Ox kidney has a very strong flavour and is mainly used in pies and puddings.

Before cooking, wash kidneys and remove skin. Cut in half on rounded side and snip out all the centre core.

Liver is a very nutritious food and perhaps the most popular offal.

Calve's liver is the best and the most expensive. Lamb's liver is a little cheaper and has a stronger flavour, but is excellent for grilling and frying, as well as in casseroles and stews. Pig's liver is usually cheaper still, but has a very strong and distinctive flavour that is not always popular. It is best stewed or casseroled and makes a very good paté. Ox liver also has a strong flavour and tends to be tough and coarse-textured. It is best casseroled or stewed.

Oxtail is usually sold jointed. The meat should be bright red with a moderate layer of firm, white fat. One oxtail with vegetables and dumplings makes a delicious stew or braise.

Sweetbreads, especially those of lamb and calf, are a much sought-after delicacy and need to be ordered in advance. The strong smell disappears during cooking. About 450 g (1 lb.) serves three or four.

Tongue is a delicacy in much demand

Lamb's Tongues with Sweet and Sour Sauce—an interesting and economical offal dish

—it may have to be ordered in advance. Both lamb's and ox tongues are popular and are available fresh or salted.

Wash thoroughly and soak in cold water. Lamb's tongues need to be soaked for one to two hours if fresh, three to four hours if salted—ox tongues two to three hours fresh, overnight if salted.

Drain the tongue and place in cold water (adding salt if the tongue is fresh) and bring to boil. Skin and add peppercorns, bay leaves and carrots. Simmer until tender, then remove, skin carefully and cut away waste.

Tripe is sold 'dressed' (cleaned and par-boiled) and only needs a thorough wash in cold water. The three kinds of tripe readily available—honeycomb, blanket and thick seam—are named after their appearances, but they taste alike. All need long, gentle cooking. Tripe is a first-class, economical food, but has little flavour of its own so additional seasonings, vegetables, or sauces are usually used. Allow 100–150 g (4–6 oz.) per person.

Ways of Serving Offal

Lamb's Tongues with Sweet and Sour Sauce

Serves 2

4 lamb's tongues
900 ml (1½ pt.) stock
Salt and pepper

Sauce

15 ml (1 level tablespoon) cornflour
150 ml (¼ pt.) cider
30 ml (2 level tablespoons) brown
    sugar
15 ml (1 tablespoon) cranberry sauce
15 ml (1 tablespoon) soy sauce
30 ml (2 tablespoons) vinegar

1. Soak tongues in cold salted water for two hours. Drain and put into a saucepan with the stock and seasoning. Cover with lid and simmer gently for about 1½ hours.
2. When cooked, skin and remove waste from tongues. Cut tongues in half, lengthwise. Replace in stock to reheat.
3. Blend the cornflour with a little of the cider. Pour into saucepan. Add the cider, brown sugar, cranberry sauce and soy sauce. Bring slowly to the boil, stirring continually, then simmer for 5–10 minutes. Add vinegar.
4. Serve with sweet and sour sauce and noodles.

Pressed Pickled Ox Tongue

Serve 100–175 g (4–6 oz.)

1 pickled ox tongue
1 onion
2 carrots
2 stalks of celery
2 bay leaves
6 peppercorns

1. Wash the tongue thoroughly and soak overnight in a large quantity of cold water.
2. Drain and put into a large pan with cold water to cover. Bring to the boil and boil for five minutes. Pour off this water, cover with fresh cold water and add the vegetables, cleaned but left whole, bay leaves and peppercorns. Bring to the boil and simmer gently until tender, removing the scum from time to time. When cooked (three to four hours), remove tongue from pan and plunge into cold water for a minute or two.
3. Skin and remove bones and waste from root end. Put the tongue, coiled round, into a press or container just big enough to hold it. Press under a very heavy weight. Leave overnight.
4. Turn out of mould and slice as required. Keep refrigerated if not all used at one time. Serve with salad.

Thick Oxtail Soup

Serves 8

450 g (1 lb.) oxtail
15 g (1 tablespoon) dripping
1 large onion
1 carrot
1 small turnip
1 small leek
10 ml (2 teaspoons) flour
10 ml (2 teaspoons) tomato purée
Bouquet garni
Salt and pepper
2 litres ($3\frac{1}{2}$ pt.) boiling water
15 ml (1 tablespoon) cornflour
Glass of sherry or red wine

1. Cut oxtail into pieces. Melt dripping in a large saucepan and lightly brown the oxtail in the hot fat.
2. Peel and halve onion and carrot. Wash and chop leek.
3. Remove meat, place vegetables in fat and brown lightly. Replace meat and add flour, tomato purée, bouquet garni, salt and pepper. Mix well. Pour in boiling water and blend. Cover and simmer for four to five hours.
4. Leave to get cold, skim off fat, remove meat from bones and cut into small pieces, replace meat in soup and bring back to the boil. Blend cornflour with a little water, add to soup and cook for five minutes, until thickened.
5. Add sherry or wine and serve immediately. Add small suet dumplings for a more substantial meal.

Heart and Vegetable Casserole

Serves 4

4 pig's or lamb's hearts
Seasoned flour
25 g (1 oz.) butter
15 ml (1 tablespoon) cooking oil
2 rashers streaky bacon
1 large onion
1 carrot
50 g (2 oz.) mushrooms
1 green pepper
150 ml ($\frac{1}{4}$ pt.) stock
150 ml ($\frac{1}{4}$ pt.) red wine
Bouquet garni
Salt and pepper

1. Wash hearts thoroughly in cold water. Trim away fat and waste and snip the wall dividing the centre. Soak for one hour in clean, salted water.
2. Prepare oven (Gas Mark 4, 350°F).
3. Rinse and drain hearts and cut into $2\frac{1}{2}$ cm (1 in.) squares and dry thoroughly. Dip in seasoned flour and fry in hot butter and oil mixed. When lightly browned place in casserole and keep warm.
4. Cut bacon into thin strips, peel and finely chop onion, peel and dice carrot, slice mushrooms, de-seed and slice pepper. Fry bacon and vegetables together in remaining butter and oil, adding in a little more if necessary. Add to hearts in casserole, pour in stock and wine and add bouquet garni and seasoning.
5. Cover and cook for one hour. Remove bouquet garni before serving. Serve with creamed potatoes.

Liver and Bacon in Tomato Sauce is a good way to present offal excitingly

Liver and Bacon in Tomato Sauce

Serves 4

700 g (1½ lb.) lamb's liver
6 rashers back bacon
1 large onion
Seasoned flour
25 g (1 oz.) butter
Salt and pepper
450 ml (¾ pt.) tomato sauce (canned)

1. Prepare oven (Gas Mark 5, 375°F). Slice liver, halve and roll bacon rashers, peel and chop onion.
2. Toss liver in the seasoned flour. Fry the onion until soft in the butter. Add liver and fry lightly on both sides.
3. Put liver and onion into a casserole. Season, then pour over tomato sauce and mix well. Put bacon rolls on top of casserole and cook, uncovered, for 30 minutes. Serve with mashed potatoes.

Stuffed Hearts

Serves 4

4 lamb's hearts
300 ml (½ pt.) stock
1 glass sherry

Stuffing

50 g (2 oz.) ham
100 g (4 oz.) fresh breadcrumbs
15 ml (1 tablespoon) chopped parsley
Pinch each of sage, rosemary, thyme
Salt and pepper
1 egg
Juice of half lemon

1. Prepare oven (Gas Mark 3, 325°F).
2. Wash hearts well in cold water. Trim fat and any waste. Cut dividing wall to make one cavity. Soak for one hour in cold salted water. Rinse well.
3. Dice ham. Mix dry stuffing ingredients together, bind with beaten

egg and lemon juice.

4. Pack stuffing well into the hearts. Put into casserole, pour over stock and cover with a tight fitting lid. Cook for $1\frac{1}{2}$ hours, basting frequently. In the last half hour of cooking add sherry.
5. Serve hearts immediately with fresh vegetables.

Liver and Bacon Casserole

Serves 4

700 g ($1\frac{1}{2}$ lb.) ox liver
1 large onion
Seasoned flour
25 g (1 oz.) butter
Salt and pepper
425 g (15 oz.) can of tomatoes
30 ml (2 tablespoons) tomato purée
6 rashers back bacon

1. Slice liver and soak in milk for one hour. Peel and chop onions.
2. Prepare oven (Gas Mark 5, 375°F). Toss liver in seasoned flour. Fry onions in butter until soft. Add liver and fry lightly on both sides. Put liver and onions in casserole and season.
3. Chop tomatoes and blend juice from can with purée. Add to casserole.
4. Cover and cook in oven for about $2\frac{1}{2}$–3 hours.
5. Roll bacon rashers, place on top in the casserole and cook, uncovered for last 30 minutes.

Sweetbreads in Breadcrumbs

Serves 3–4

450 g (1 lb.) lamb's sweetbreads

300 ml ($\frac{1}{2}$ pt.) water
Juice of half lemon
1 egg
60 ml (4 tablespoons) breadcrumbs
15 ml (1 tablespoon) chopped parsley
Salt and pepper
50 g (2 oz.) butter
Lemon slices

1. Wash sweetbreads and soak in cold water for one hour.
2. Drain and put into a saucepan with the fresh cold water and lemon juice. Cover and simmer for 15 minutes.
3. Drain and remove sinews and outside membranes. Flatten sweetbreads between two plates with a weight on top for one hour.
4. Dip the sweetbreads in beaten egg and coat in breadcrumbs and chopped parsley mixed together with seasoning.
5. Fry gently in butter. Serve immediately with lemon slices.

Liver and Kidney Kebabs

Serves 4

225 g (8 oz.) lamb's liver
4 lamb's kidneys
8 mushrooms
4 tomatoes
Cooking oil

1. Cut liver into cubes. Skin, core and quarter kidneys. Halve tomatoes.
2. Thread ingredients onto four skewers, starting and finishing with tomato. Brush well with oil and put under a hot grill. Turn frequently while cooking.
3. Serve on a bed of boiled rice with a side salad.

Oxtail Braise

Serves 3–4

15 ml (1 tablespoon) dripping
1 oxtail
3 small onions
3 small carrots
3 sticks of celery
2 leeks
15 ml (1 tablespoon) flour
Bouquet garni
Salt and pepper
600 ml (1 pt.) stock

1. Prepare oven (Gas Mark 4, 350°F). Melt the dripping in a flameproof casserole. Brown oxtail lightly in hot fat.
2. Peel and quarter onions and carrots, wash and cut celery and leeks into pieces.
3. Remove meat from fat, add vegetables and brown lightly. Replace meat and add flour, bouquet garni, salt and pepper. Pour in stock and blend with fat and flour.
4. Cover and cook in oven for four hours.

Tripe Catalene

Serves 4

450 g (1 lb.) tripe
1 large onion
4 tomatoes
25 g (1 oz.) butter
1 clove garlic
5 ml (1 teaspoon) mixed herbs
5 ml (1 teaspoon) parsley
Pinch grated nutmeg
Salt and pepper
150 ml ($\frac{1}{4}$ pt.) white wine

1. Boil the tripe until tender and then cut into fine strips.
2. Peel and finely chop onion. Skin and chop tomatoes.
3. Melt butter, add onion and fry until soft. Add tripe, tomatoes and crushed garlic, mixed herbs, parsley, nutmeg, salt and pepper. Fry for five minutes.
4. Add white wine and cook, covered, until all ingredients are tender. Serve with sauté potatoes.

Brains on Toast

Serves 2

2 sets lamb's brains
300 ml ($\frac{1}{2}$ pt.) stock
5 ml (1 tablespoon) vinegar
1 onion
25 g (1 oz.) butter
30 ml (2 tablespoons) white wine
Salt and pepper
2 slices toast
Paprika

1. Soak brains in cold, salted water for one hour.
2. Remove skin and any traces of blood. Simmer in stock and vinegar for 15 minutes. Drain and plunge into very cold water. Allow brains to cool in water. Drain.
3. Peel and chop onion, then fry in butter until soft. Put to one side of pan. Add brains and break up into small pieces; fry until browned. Mix in with the onion. Add wine and seasoning. Cook for a further five minutes.
4. Serve on toast with paprika sprinkled over.

Rabbit

Shopping for Rabbit

Rabbits, of course, have been available on the meat market for a long time, although the demand for them diminished during the outbreak of the disease myxomatosis in the 1950s and 1960s. In recent years, with the cost of meat increasing alarmingly, demand has risen again and farmed rabbits have offered a welcome change and a relatively inexpensive meat.

If you are keeping rabbits yourself you will know exactly how old they are, but if you are buying from a butcher you will want to know how to judge the animal's age.

Young rabbits have long, pointed claws and small white teeth, while older rabbits have rough, rounded claws and long, yellow front teeth. Choose short-necked, plump animals, with firm, undiscoloured flesh.

Strangely, wild rabbits are often preferred to farmed rabbits, as they are said to have a better flavour, though the flesh of the farmed rabbits is white and more delicate.

A rabbit should be paunched (that is, the 'innards' removed) before it is hung, though hanging should not be for more than a day. This will normally have been done for you, of course.

The traditional season for rabbits is September to March, though nowadays the use of frozen imported animals means rabbit can be enjoyed all the year round.

Ways of Serving Rabbit

Stewed Rabbit with Onion Sauce

Serves 3–4

1 rabbit
Seasoning
Herbs (mixed)
50 g (2 oz.) ham
3 onions
25 g (1 oz.) flour
25 g (1 oz.) butter

1. Clean and wash the rabbit well. Dry and cut into joints. Place in a saucepan with cold water to cover. Bring to boil then pour water away and rinse both the saucepan and rabbit. This will whiten the flesh.
2. Cover again with warm water. Add the seasoning, herbs, chopped ham and chopped onions. Replace the lid and cook slowly for about 30 minutes, or until the rabbit is tender. Strain off liquid, retaining it to make the sauce.
3. Blend the flour with the melted butter and cook for one minute. Add the cooking stock, bring to the boil, stirring and simmer for five minutes, then pour over rabbit pieces.

Rabbit Hotpot

Serves 4–5

1 rabbit
450 g (1 lb.) neck of mutton
15 ml (1 tablespoon) flour
Salt and pepper
450 g (1 lb.) onions
900 g (2 lb.) potatoes
150 ml ($\frac{1}{4}$ pt.) stock
300 ml ($\frac{1}{2}$ pt.) milk

1. Prepare oven (Gas Mark 4, 350°F).
2. Cut rabbit into joints, wash in salted water and blanch, as described for Stewed Rabbit.
3. Cut mutton into neat pieces.
4. Mix flour, salt and pepper together and coat pieces of rabbit and mutton.
5. Peel and finely slice onions and potatoes and place a layer in bottom of casserole.
6. Season and cover with mutton pieces, then arrange rabbit over this. Top with remainder of onion and potatoes. Pour over stock and milk.
7. Cook for about $2\frac{1}{2}$ hours until the flesh is tender.

Accompaniments and Flavouring

There are many ways in which good flavouring can be achieved in meat cookery. The use of vegetables, spices, herbs and condiments does much to give a good savoury flavour.

Let's examine some of the main ingredients that go well with meat. Salt and pepper are essential. Pepper is best bought in the form of peppercorns and ground in a pepper mill when required. Use white pepper for a 'hot' taste and black for 'spicy/pungent' taste.

Herbs can be used extensively and imaginatively in meat dishes. Buy good quality dried herbs, or if you are ambitious try growing your own! Parsley and mint are easy to grow and can be used in many recipes. Parsley is particularly good for garnishing. Other herbs that go well with meat are sage, thyme, bay leaves, basil, rosemary, chives, marjoram and tarragon. Essential for stocks and stews is a bouquet garni. These can be purchased or you can make your own. Put sprigs of parsley and thyme and a crushed bay leaf in muslin or kitchen paper, tie with string and place in with the stew. Remove before serving.

Some spices useful for meat cookery are cloves, nutmeg, mace, coriander and allspice. Curry powder gives a particularly recognisable flavour, but it can be used in small amounts in some dishes to give an extra 'spiciness'.

Tomato purée and canned tomatoes are a worthwhile buy. They can often be cheaper than the fresh product and have a much stronger flavour. Onions are a common ingredient in stews and braises. Use Spanish for a mild flavour and English for a stronger taste. Shallots and small pickling onions are good too, and spring onions give a delicate flavour. Garlic is an acquired taste, but for many classic dishes it is essential.

Cooking liquor or stock can be home-made or from a purchased cube. Whichever you use, make sure it is well-flavoured. To make an ordinary dish into something more special, try mixing the stock with a little wine, cider or beer.

Other ingredients useful in meat cookery are Worcester sauce, hot pepper sauce, soy sauce, pickles, grated lemon and orange rind and wine vinegar.

To introduce extra flavour and tenderness to meat that is to be grilled or roasted, steep it in a marinade. Wine vinegar, Worcester sauce, oil, garlic, lemon juice and soy sauce can be used in varying proportions, again with wine, cider or beer.

Put the meat in a polythene bag, add the marinade and leave for one to two hours or overnight in the refrigerator. The marinade can be used for basting during cooking.

Table 6.   Accompaniments and Flavourings

Meat	Traditional accompaniment
Roast Beef	Yorkshire pudding. Mustard. Horseradish sauce. Thin gravy
Roast Lamb	Mint sauce. Thin gravy
Roast Mutton	Redcurrant jelly. Onion sauce. Thin gravy
Roast Pork	Sage and onion stuffing. Apple sauce. Thick gravy
Roast Veal	Veal forcemeat. Bacon rolls. Thick gravy
Grilled Meat } Fried Meat	Maitre d'hotel butter. Grilled tomatoes and mushrooms. Matchstick potatoes. Watercress. Worcester sauce With pork and bacon—pineapple rings
Boiled Beef	Dumplings. Vegetables cooked with meat and cooking liquor
Boiled Mutton	As above and caper sauce
Boiled Bacon	As above and parsley sauce
Braised Meats	Vegetables cooked with meat and reduced or thickened cooking liquor
Brown Stew	Vegetables cooked with meat. Thickened cooking liquid. Potatoes, rice or noodles. Chopped parsley
'White' Stews	Bacon rolls, mushrooms, lemon slices. Thickened cooking liquid. Deep fried croûtons

Leftovers

Leftover meat should be kept in one piece, covered and stored in a cool place for not longer than two days. To prepare for re-heating, remove any bone and use for stock. Trim away all skin and gristle as this will become tough on re-heating.

When used the meat should be cut in small pieces or better still passed through a mincer. When mincing, it's a good idea to pass a dry bread crust through the mincer at the end to clear it of any meat shreds. It is important that the meat is finely divided so there is quick penetration of heat.

Additional ingredients such as onion or potato, which may be added, must be cooked, or partially cooked, as re-heating does not allow time for cooking.

As moisture and flavour have been lost during the first cooking, these must be added to a re-heated dish. Moisture can be added as sauces, stock, gravy and so on. Seasonings and flavourings, such as herbs, curry powder and vegetables add flavour. Try also to add milk, eggs and cheese, as they not only add flavour but also nutritive value.

Re-heat meat quickly, so that it reaches a safe temperature, Gas Mark 5 (375°F), as soon as possible. Bacteria multiply rapidly in a warm, moist mixture and this *must* be avoided. Don't re-cook the dish as this will toughen the meat fibres, so bring up to temperature but don't allow to heat for too long.

It is a good idea to protect the food from this possible re-cooking and this can be done in several ways:
(a) Topping with potatoes—as in shepherd's pie.
(b) Dipping in batter—as in meat fritters.
(c) Sealing in pastry—as in meat pasties.
(d) Coating in egg and breadcrumbs—as in rissoles.

Make a special effort when serving and garnishing re-heated dishes, as they can become boring. Serve in attractive dishes, possibly individual. Garnish with brightly coloured foods such as tomatoes or parsley and add something with extra 'bite' such as croûtons or crusty bread.

Re-heated dishes lack vitamin C so always serve with freshly-cooked vegetables or plan a fresh fruit dessert. The last and most important thing to remember is that meat must never be re-heated a second time.

Stock

The bones removed from cooked joints can be used for stock. Remove fat and any scraps of meat and put them with the bones into a large saucepan. Cover with cold water and $2\frac{1}{2}$ ml ($\frac{1}{2}$ teaspoon) salt to each 600 ml (1 pt.) of water.

Bring to the boil, cover and simmer gently for about two hours. Add raw diced vegetables such as onion, carrot and celery and simmer for a further hour.

Strain the stock and cool as quickly as possible. Do not keep stock longer than a day in a larder and no longer than two days in the refrigerator. Stock can be a good breeding ground for bacteria. Always use each batch of stock up completely, never add new to old.

The fat can be skimmed from the stock while still warm, or allowed to set and removed at this stage.

Dripping

When roasting a joint, extra fat or dripping always collects in the pan. This can be kept and used for frying, but to improve its keeping quality it should be clarified.

To clarify dripping, melt the fat and strain into a basin. Take two to three times as much boiling water and pour over the dripping. Stir and then leave to cool. The clean fat will rise to the top and can be lifted off when it has solidified.

Scrape off any sediment remaining underneath.

Table 7.   Oven Temperatures

Oven	Gas Mark	°F	°C	Oven	Gas Mark	°F	°C
Very cool	1	275	140	Fairly hot	6	400	200
Cool	2	300	150	Hot	7	425	220
Warm	3	325	170	Very hot	8	450	230
Moderately warm	4	350	180	Very hot	9	475	240
Fairly hot	5	375	190				